AIR RAID PRECAUTIONS

AIR RAID PRECAUTIONS

Edited by Campbell McCutcheon

TEMPUS

First published 1938, this edition 2007

Tempus Publishing
Cirencester Road, Chalford
Stroud, Gloucestershire, GL6 8PE
www.tempus-publishing.com

Tempus Publishing is an imprint of NPI Media Group

British Library Cataloguing in Publication Data.
A catalogue record for this book is available from the British Library.

ISBN 978 0 7524 4470 3

Typesetting and origination by NPI Media Group
Printed and bound in Great Britain

Introduction

Zeppelins were the threat from the sky during the First World War. These big, lumbering, hydrogen-filled airships were not capable of vast speeds or of carrying huge quantities of bombs, but for the first time they brought the concept of total war to the British Isles. For those unlucky enough to live on the East Coast, Zeppelin attacks were a common threat. The airships weren't invulnerable and a few were shot down during the war. Despite having long-range Gotha bombers, the Germans still did not have aircraft capable of carrying a load of bombs to England and dropping them. That wasn't to say that attack by bombers didn't happen. The Germans introduced the cunning concept of seaplanes that were towed by submarine to the shores of England and then used to bomb coastal towns. However, by the war's end, England had seen little in the way of attack on its civilian population. That was all to change during the next war.

To battle-harden and train their pilots and troops, the Germans sent many men to Spain during the Civil War. Fighting on Franco's Nationalist side against the Republicans, the German soldiers and airmen had the opportunity to practise total warfare for the first time. On 26 April 1937, twenty-four German and Italian planes descended on Guernica, dropping almost 25 tons of bombs on the town, destroying much of it. It was one of the first ever instances of carpet-bombing a town into submission. Casualties were huge, with estimates varying from 300 to over 1,500.

The world's governments took note. No longer was the civilian population safe from the effects of war – the war was as likely to come to them now. Preparations were made, advice was collected and collated into the little booklet The Protection of Your Home Against Air Raids, and a copy sent to every household in the country. This small 36pp booklet gave basic advice on what to do to prepare yourself for war, and what to do if war came. It was issued in March 1938, at the same time as gas masks started to be given to every man, woman and child in the country. Neville Chamberlain's visit to Munich was still six months ahead but almost everyone feared war was coming: and everyone now knew what war meant for the civilian population. Municipal air-raid shelters began to be constructed all over the country, and cigarette companies such as Wills and Players issued cigarette card sets entitled Air Raid Precautions, full of handy guides on what to do in the event of an attack by air. Although banned, the thought of an attack using poison gas was so great that, later in 1938, Air Raid Precautions: Personal Protection against Gas was published and many thousands were trained in what to do in the unlikely event of attack by gas.

By July 1939, it was no longer a case of if war should come, but when war shall come. In this month a series of four public information leaflets were issued to every household in the land. On 1 September, Hitler invaded

Poland and Britain and France issued an ultimatum that would lead to the declaration of war only two days later. British troops were rushed to support France's borders with Germany and the first RAF sorties, a photographic reconnaissance over Wilhelmshaven, took place on 3 September. It was not until 29 November that the first German bomber was shot down over the Lothians in Scotland. Strangely, some of the first UK air raids were on the Forth Bridge and at Lerwick in the Shetlands where six Heinkel HE111s failed to cause any real damage to their intended targets of shipping in the harbour.

Beyond the odd skirmish, there was little evidence of the air war over Britain until the summer of 1940. Both Britain and Germany were building up reserves of aircraft and munitions in preparation for what lay ahead. In the UK, factories were camouflaged, a blackout was imposed and the civilian population evacuated from potential target areas. With Hitler preoccupied with the invasion of Denmark and Norway in May 1940, there was little activity on the Western Front with the period from September 1939 to the end of the month being known as the Phoney War. Men and material were still being ploughed into France, ready for the expected invasion of that country. On 16 May, Air Chief Marshall Dowding wrote to the Prime Minister demanding that no more RAF fighter squadrons should go to France. His foresight most likely helped save Britain during the conflict that was to come. By the end of the month, France was overrun, over 300,000 troops had been evacuated from Dunkirk and a host of other ports in northern and western France and Britain stood alone.

Hitler began to collect the barges and ships required for the proposed invasion of England in the Channel ports. RAF skirmishes helped destroy some of these but for a month the population waited for the proposed invasion. Hermann Goering, the head of the Luftwaffe, promised to annihilate the RAF and on 10 July the period known as the Battle of Britain began. It was a matter of life and death and as long as the RAF held air supremacy over Britain, the invasion could not take place. For a month most attacks were on the RAF's airfields, radar stations and aircraft factories, but in August the focus was shifted to the civilian population. For many in towns and cities such as London, Coventry, Clydebank, Birmingham, Bristol, Portsmouth and Southampton, their Air Raid Precautions books were to prove immensely useful. Saved from the peril of attack by poison gas, nevertheless the civilian population endured five years of attack from the air. Until early 1942 the attacks were relentless but, as Allied aircraft gained air supremacy at night, they became less frequent, with attacks by lone bombers more prevalent than that by masses of aircraft . By June 1944 the danger was no longer from bombers but the V1 and V2 jet and rocket bombs.

Of course, by the end of May 1945, the war was over in Europe, and many people consigned their Air Raid Precautions books to the rubbish tip. Printed in their millions, it is surprising how few have survived to the present day, but those that have give an insight into life in Britain during the dark days at the start of the war. Together for the very first time, we bring a variety of the official publications on Air Raid Precautions. Primarily designed for the householder, we have included some of the pamphlets designed for Air Raid Wardens too.

Why this book has been sent to you

If this country were ever at war the target of the enemy's bombers would be the staunchness of the people at home. We all hope and work to prevent war but, while there is risk of it, we cannot afford to neglect the duty of preparing ourselves and the country for such an emergency. This book is being sent out, in the first place, for the use of air raid wardens and other volunteers in the air raid precautions services, and of the servants of the local authorities who are undertaking air raid precautions duties.

At the present moment one of the most important tasks is to help each householder to realise what he can do, if the need arose, to make his home and his household more safe against air attack.

The Home Office is working with the local authorities in preparing schemes for the protection of the civil population during an attack. But it is impossible to devise a scheme that will cover everybody unless each home and family play their part in doing what they can for themselves. In this duty to themselves they must count upon the help and advice of those who have undertaken the duty of advice and instruction.

If the emergency comes the country will look for her safety not only to her sailors and soldiers and airmen, but also to the organised courage and foresight of every household. It is for the volunteers in the air raid precautions services to help every household for this purpose, and in sending out this book I ask for their help.

Samuel Hoare

March, 1938.

CONTENTS

THINGS TO DO NOW

On board ship, both crew and passengers are instructed where to go and what to do, not when danger threatens, but beforehand. The captain considers it a matter of ordinary routine and everyday precaution that everything is in readiness for a shipwreck which he hopes will never happen. If the head of the house will consider himself as " the captain of the ship " and put these air raid precautions into effect, the principal object of this book will have been achieved.

IF air raids ever came to this country, every home should have a refuge specially prepared in which the whole household could take cover in greater safety. Every shop and office, or other place of work or business, would require a place similarly prepared for those engaged on the premises.

Every householder, or head of a family or business, should learn now how to protect, in war-time, his own people and home from the effects of explosive bombs, incendiary bombs, and poison gas.

This applies chiefly to those who live in large centres of population. In more remote districts the dangers would be very much less, though the need for some protection and precautions would still exist.

All the precautions recommended in this book are useful. Most of them can be adopted to some extent by everyone. The essential things cost little to do, and some of the more elaborate ones you will find you can do quite easily, either yourself or by combining with a neighbour, if you decide to begin NOW, and take your time.

Do not hesitate to ask a friend or a neighbour, or an air raid warden, to help you if you feel you need advice. A local air raid precautions organisation has been, or will be, established in your district and expert help and information are already available. For any further advice about what you should do, apply in the first instance to your local Council Offices.

WHAT TO DO NOW

The whole of this book is concerned with how to counter the danger of air attack. It is divided into sections so that you can turn quickly to any part and find out exactly what to do in any emergency. So please keep it carefully. But first read it through. Then come back to this page and think over these things:

1 Decide, according to the instructions given on page 8, what place would make the best refuge-room for your household at home, and begin to plan now how you would get it ready.

2 If you are in charge of a business or shop, or an hotel or lodging house, or of tenements, decide upon places of refuge for those for whose safety and welfare you would be responsible.

3 Study carefully the precautions you can take against fire, and especially the instructions for dealing with a small incendiary bomb.

4 In time of war all buildings will have to be completely darkened at night. Be ready to do this for your home.

5 *Begin* to collect :—
>   materials for gas-protecting your refuge-room ;
>   materials for darkening your whole house or business premises ;
>   the things you would need in your refuge-room ;
>   simple fire appliances, if you can afford them.

6 If you live in a large town, think whether you can make arrangements for children, invalids and elderly persons, and pets, to be sent away the moment danger threatens, so that they may be in a place of greater safety.

7 Find out from your local Council Offices the air raid precautions organisation and the emergency fire brigade arrangements being prepared in your district. Keep yourself familiar with the protective measures that the Government and the Local Authorities are taking.

>   *Most important of all, see that all grown-ups are familiar with the contents of this book and know of the arrangements you are making for their safety. Do not do nothing, either on the ground that there is no need, or because you think that nothing you can do will be of any avail. Your safety, and the safety of those for whom you are responsible, may depend on you.*

Darkening the house at night

It is vital that raiders should not see the lights of a town at night; so vital that the Government might order the darkening of all buildings even before war broke out. So you must be ready to darken every window, skylight, glass door or exterior opening in parts of the house where lights are used after dark. You will need dark blinds, thick curtains, or some heavy material that will cover the windows completely. Material which lets anyone outside see that there is a light inside will not do. Bear this in mind when you next buy blinds and curtains. Skylights, fanlights and glass doors can best be covered with black paint or thick paper. If necessary get these things now, because in an emergency the shops might be quickly sold out.

RESPIRATORS

The Government is making arrangements to provide respirators free to the civilian population in all districts where they might be needed. But regard your respirator as your *second line* of defence and the precautions advised in this book as your *first*.

What a respirator is

A respirator, if properly put on, protects the eyes, nose, mouth and lungs; and ensures a supply of *pure* air for breathing, by means of filters which are able to absorb any gas known to be capable of being used in war. The facepiece, the edges of which fit closely round the face, prevents any air from getting inside the respirator except that which passes through the filters. It is held in position by adjustable straps behind the head. Once these straps have been properly adjusted, the respirator, if needed, can be put on instantly.

How a respirator works

A respirator consists of a rubber facepiece with a transparent window, and a container which holds the gas filters. There are two filters, one of which consists of specially prepared charcoal, and the other of pads of specially prepared material. The illus-

THE CIVILIAN RESPIRATOR

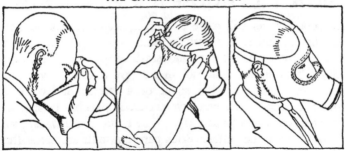

Putting it on   Adjusting the head straps

tration shows the type of respirator which has been designed for you by Government experts. Although simple to look at, exhaustive tests have shown it to be highly efficient.

But these war respirators do not afford protection against ordinary domestic coal gas or carbon monoxide, which cannot be used as war gases.

Why a respirator alone is not enough

Your refuge-room is your first line of defence because a respirator cannot protect the other parts of your body from dangerous liquids, such as " mustard gas." These liquid " gases " need the most rigorous precautions, because they continue to be dangerous long after they have been dropped. The vapour as well as the liquid affects the skin of parts of the body not protected by the respirator. Remember, too, that by staying in a refuge-room you have some protection against flying splinters and débris, as well as additional protection against gas.

Your respirator will not be issued unless it becomes necessary, but will be carefully stored in readiness to be distributed very quickly before an actual emergency came. Arrangements will, however, be made to enable you to try a respirator on, and to get used to wearing it beforehand, if you want to. Children can wear respirators. For those too young to wear them a special means of protection will be provided. A respirator is not uncomfortable to wear, and you can see and hear and speak when wearing it.

HOW TO CHOOSE A REFUGE-ROOM

Almost any room will serve as a refuge-room if it is soundly constructed, and if it is easy to reach and to get out of. Its windows should be as few and small as possible, preferably facing a building or blank wall, or a narrow street. If a ground floor room facing a wide street or a stretch of level open ground is chosen, the windows should if possible be specially protected (see pages 30 and 31). The stronger the walls, floor, and ceiling are, the better. Brick partition walls are better than lath and plaster, a concrete ceiling is better than a wooden one. An internal passage will form a very good refuge-room if it can be closed at both ends.

The best floor for a refuge-room

A cellar or basement is the best place for a refuge-room if it can be made reasonably gas-proof and if there is no likelihood of its becoming flooded by a neighbouring river that may burst its banks, or by a burst water-main. If you have any doubt about the risk of flooding ask for advice from your local Council Offices.

A cellar or basement is the best position for a refuge-room if it can be made reasonably gas-proof

Alternatively, any room on any floor below the top floor may be used. Top floors and attics should be avoided as they usually do not give sufficient protection overhead from small incendiary bombs. These small bombs are capable of piercing the roof, but are unlikely to get below the top floor when they first fall.

In a house with only two floors and without a cellar, choose a room on the ground floor so that you have protection overhead

In flats or tenement houses, either each household can make its own arrangements or communal refuges can be made. It is, however, important that top-floor dwellers should find accommodation downstairs. They might share a refuge-room, or they might make arrangements to occupy the basement. But the basement premises will have to be prepared as refuges in the same way as ordinary rooms, according to the instructions given in this book.

In a two-storeyed terrace house choose a room on the ground floor. The flanking walls will protect you from the blast of a bursting bomb

It is suggested that in any flat, or tenement house, or house occupied by more than one family, representatives be chosen and formed into a Protection Committee to decide upon the most suitable rooms and to prepare them as refuge-rooms if it should ever be necessary for the safety of all.

Even though your household occupies one room only, many of the precautions recommended in the book can still be carried out, and will help to protect you. So do what you can.

How large should a refuge-room be ?

Although an actual raid may be over in a few minutes it might be necessary to stay in your refuge-room for some time, even perhaps for several hours, until the gas in the neighbourhood has been cleared away. You should therefore know how many persons can remain safely in one room without suffering any ill effects. For rooms of normal height (8 to 10 feet) an allowance of 20 square feet of floor area for each person will enable those persons to remain in the room with complete safety for a continuous period of twelve hours *without ventilation*.

A room 10 ft. × 10 ft. will hold 5 persons.
A room 15 ft. × 10 ft. will hold 7 persons.
A room 20 ft. × 12 ft. will hold 12 persons.

IF YOU CANNOT SPECIALLY SET ASIDE A ROOM FOR A REFUGE-ROOM

You can still make a refuge-room even if you have no surplus room to set aside, in war-time, specially for the purpose. If you have only one room you can make it a place of greater safety— even if you adopt only some of the suggestions contained in this book. Do not think you have no protection. Any room within solid walls is safer than being out in the open, so don't run out into the street to find better shelter if you ever get an air raid warning.

GET THESE THINGS FOR THE REFUGE-ROOM

These are some of the things that will be useful in your refuge-room. Keep them in mind and begin collecting those things you haven't got, one by one. Put them in a box, or in a drawer, in the room you have chosen for your refuge-room.

Things you probably possess already

Candles and matches	Old newspaper and brown paper
Hammer and nails	Some clean rags
Scissors	Needles, cotton, and thread

Things to collect

A candle lamp, or an electric hand lamp

Suitable material (see page 16) to protect the windows from the blast of an explosion

Gummed paper and adhesive tape

A few tins or jars with air-tight lids for storing food

A bottle of disinfectant

A box of First Aid Supplies : see page 19

A list of *additional* things to get into your refuge-room, if there should ever be a war, is given on page 18.

If you have a wireless set or receiver it would be useful to have it in the refuge-room so that you could hear the news and pass the time away. Make sure that the plug for it, and the leads for the aerial and earth, if these are required, are made ready.

THINGS TO DO IF THERE SHOULD EVER BE A WAR

The Government will tell you when, if ever, you should take the precautions recommended in this section. There is no need to do any of these things now, but read through these notes carefully, bearing in mind that they are intended to be nothing more than notes. Think them out, and see how to apply them to your own home. You will know, then, more exactly what to do if there should ever be a war. Having faced the problem before danger threatens you will have your plans made, and be ready to carry them out quickly if ever there is need.

IFever you receive warning that war threatens, do these things at once :—

1 *Prepare and equip your refuge-room.*

2 *Make all preparations for darkening the house at night. Windows, skylights, fanlights, glazed doors must be completely obscured.*

3 *Clear the loft, attic, top floor, of inflammable stuff that can be moved, to lessen the risk of fire from an incendiary bomb that might penetrate the roof. Assemble appliances to fight fires. Also, if possible, limewash the timbers in the attic or roof space.*

4 *If you live in a large town, children, invalids, elderly members of the household, and pets, should be sent to relatives or friends in the country, if this is possible.*

DARKEN YOUR HOUSE AT NIGHT

All windows, skylights, fanlights, glazed doors, or other openings in parts of the house where lights are used, must be completely screened after dusk, so that no light is visible from outside.

If blinds are used alone, they must be of stout material and dark in colour and must cover the window completely. If curtains are used they must be dark and thick. Dark blankets or carpets or thick sheets of brown paper can be used to cover windows temporarily.

Special care must be taken to cover completely skylights and other windows directly visible from the air.

All lights near an outside door must be screened so that no light can be seen when the door is opened. Outside lights, garden and porch lights, must not be used. If they are electric, take the bulbs out altogether.

HOW TO PREPARE YOUR REFUGE-ROOM
against the entry of gas

No serious amount of gas will come into a room unless there are draughts or currents of air to carry it in, so any cracks or openings must be sealed up somehow.

How to deal with cracks in walls, floors, and odd places

In old houses especially, windows and doors may shut badly. There may be chinks underneath the window sills on the inside. There may be cracks in the ceiling. The illustration below shows you the kind of places to look for. If possible make good these faults now without waiting for a war emergency.

Fill in all cracks and crevices with putty or a pulp made of sodden newspaper. Paste paper over any cracks in the walls or ceiling. Fill in, or paste paper over, the cracks between the floor boards ; or, better still, paste sheets of paper over the whole floor. If the floor is already covered with linoleum or an all-over carpet, do not take it up, but pay attention to any cracks or joins there may be. Fill in all cracks round the skirting boards, or where pipes pass through the walls. All trap-doors, skylights and

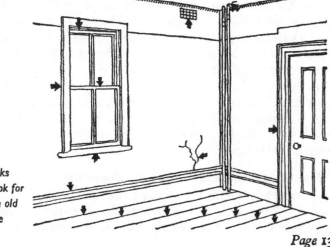

Cracks to look for in an old house

hatches in the room should be sealed, and interior ventilators stopped up with rags or pasted over with thick paper.

All ventilators in the outside walls of the house, including those below the floor level, should be stopped up with rags or paper.

If there is a fire-place, stuff the chimney with paper, rags, or sacks. Do not, of course, light a fire in the grate afterwards. Seal the front of the fire-place with a sheet of plywood and adhesive tape.

Plug key-holes. Plug waste-pipes, or overflow pipes, in any basin or sink in your refuge-room. If you are doubtful whether a hole or a crack lets in air, play for safety, and seal it up.

You can still use the room, for ordinary living purposes, provided you can do without a fire. If a fire is necessary, be ready to put it out quickly, and to seal the chimney and fire-place.

How to seal the windows of your refuge-room

The windows should be sealed so that draughts, or gas, cannot come in. Wedge them firmly to keep them tightly fixed in their frames. Seal all round the frames with gummed strip or pasted paper, wherever there is a crack. Be cautious, and make a thorough job of it. Any broken panes should be boarded in, or the holes pasted over with strong paper. This will not prevent the possibility of glass being broken by the blast of a bomb explosion, perhaps quite a long way away. So protect the glass if possible, in one of the ways suggested on page 16.

Be ready to reseal the window openings if the glass gets broken. For this purpose have some stout materials to hang or fasten over them. Use a close-woven material, or a blind, for instance, if it is large enough. Fasten it by nailing it with thin strips of wood to the window frame all round, and then seal the edges with adhesive tape.

How to seal the doors in your refuge-room

Doors to the refuge-room which need not be used should be sealed. Paper should be pasted firmly all round the cracks, especially at the foot of the door, and the key-hole plugged.

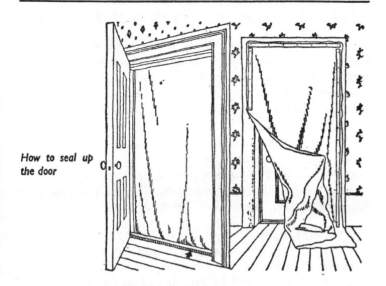

How to seal up the door

Doors which have to be opened and closed should be sealed against gas. This is how to do it.

Nail a piece of wood, padded with felt, to the floor so that the door, when closed, presses tightly against it. Take care not to nail this piece of wood on the wrong side of the door so that it cannot be opened. Strips of felt may also be nailed round the inside of the door to exclude draughts. Fix a blanket outside the door if the door opens inwards, or inside the door if the door opens outwards, with strips of wood. The top of the blanket should be fixed to the top of the door frame. One side of the blanket should be fastened down the whole length of the door frame, on the side where the hinges are, by means of a strip of wood nailed to the frame. The other side of the blanket should be secured not more than two feet down, so that a flap is left free for going in and out. Arrange the blanket so that at least 12 inches trails on the floor to stop air from blowing underneath it. See illustration above. If the blanket is kept damp during an air raid, it will give better protection.

HOW TO PREPARE YOUR REFUGE-ROOM
against the effect of explosive bombs

There are three main types of bomb, an explosive bomb, an incendiary bomb, a gas bomb. Precautions against fire are described on page 20 and the way to deal with incendiary bombs and fires generally on pages 26 and 27, under the heading " What to do if fire breaks out." How to protect yourself against gas has already been explained. How to provide some protection against explosive bombs is dealt with here.

The essential thing is to protect your refuge-room against the shock of a bomb that may burst some distance away, and from flying glass and splinters caused by the explosion.

Protecting the windows of the refuge-room

Unless a window is barricaded with sandbags in the way described on page 30, it is not easy to prevent the glass of closed windows being shattered by the blast of an explosion, even at some distance away. But you can prevent splinters of glass being blown into the room by covering the inside of the window panes with at least two thin sheets of one of the transparent or translucent, non-inflammable materials now commonly used for wrapping purposes. The material must be tough and not readily torn. Although a cellulose varnish is the best adhesive, ordinary gum can be used to stick the material to the glass, but examine it from time to time and regum when necessary.

Thin celluloid makes a better job, but a non-inflammable variety should be used, and it requires a cellulose varnish to stick it to the window pane. The moisture-proof variety of transparent wrapping material, such as is used on food packets and so on, also requires a cellulose varnish as an adhesive.

Failing anything better, some fabric material such as linen from old pillow cases, or mosquito netting, or even stout paper, may be pasted on the inside of the glass ; but these materials are not so effective as transparent wrapping material, or celluloid ; and they reduce the light.

Strengthening the room

If your refuge-room is on the ground floor or in the basement, you can support the ceiling with wooden props as an additional protection. The illustration shows a way of doing this. Stout posts or scaffold poles are placed upright, resting on a thick plank on the floor and supporting a stout piece of timber against the ceiling, at right angles to the ceiling joists.

How to support a ceiling

The illustration below shows the detail of how to fix the props

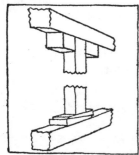

The smaller illustration shows how the posts are held in position at the top by two blocks of wood on the ceiling beam. The posts are forced tight by two wedges at the foot, driven in opposite ways. Do not drive these wedges too violently, otherwise you may lift the ceiling and damage it. If the floor of your refuge-room is solid, such as you might find in a basement, you will not need a plank across the whole floor, but only a piece of wood a foot or so long under each prop.

THINGS TO HAVE IN YOUR REFUGE-ROOM

Get these additional things into your refuge-room, as soon as the Government warns you of a threat of war. The list given on page 10 is of things to collect for your refuge-room in advance.

A roll-call list of all who should be present. This applies particularly to office premises, or if the refuge-room is to be shared by neighbours

Tables and chairs; plates, cups, knives, forks, etc.

Plenty of water for drinking, washing and fire fighting

Tinned food, with a tin-opener

A food chest of some kind (airtight tins or jars will do) to protect other food against contact with gas

Washhand-stand, or basin; washing things, soap, towels

Chamber pots, toilet-paper; disinfectant; a screen for privacy

Books, writing materials, cards; toys for the children

A simple hand-pump, and sand with a long-handled shovel

Spare blankets or rugs for resealing the window if it should be blown in

Gummed paper, or pots of paste or gum, for pasting paper over cracks and window panes. Paste can be made from flour and water boiled with a few cloves to keep it fresh

You may also like to have the following things which, if you are using them in other parts of the house, you should take into your refuge-room when you hear the air raid warning.

A mattress, or mattresses, to lie on

Overcoats, blankets, eiderdowns, rugs and warm coverings

The wireless set, gramophone with records

Mackintoshes, goloshes, gum boots

An electric kettle is useful if you have one, but don't burn a gas fire or gas ring, as it uses up air.

If the weather is really cold, you may use an electric fire in your refuge-room for a while if you wish. But the air will remain much fresher if you can avoid artificial heating of any kind. It is better to rely on coats and blankets for warmth.

MAKE IN THE SPACE BELOW A LIST
of any other things which occur to you as
worth getting for your own refuge-room

SIMPLE FIRST AID SUPPLIES

You should have, as suggested in the list on page 10, a few first
aid supplies for your refuge-room. The list of articles below is
about right for a household of six or seven persons all sheltering
in one room. For hints on how to use them, see Section 5
at the end of the book.

3 1-oz. packets of lint, for dressing wounds
3 1-oz. packets of cotton wool, for pads on dressings
2 triangular bandages, for use as arm-slings or, when folded,
      as bandages
3 1-in. roller bandages, for fingers
3 2½-in. roller bandages, for head or limbs
3 3-in. roller bandages, for limbs or body
Stout string or cord for stopping an artery from bleeding
1 dozen small safety pins
1 pair of scissors
1 bottle of smelling salts
Sal volatile
Iodine, or antiseptic

PRECAUTIONS AGAINST FIRE

An air attack may include the use of large numbers of small incendiary bombs. So many fires might be started that the fire brigades could not deal with them, and every citizen must be prepared to help. Do these things the moment you receive official warning that war threatens.

1 Clear the loft, attic, or top floor of all inflammable material, paper, litter, lumber, etc., to lessen the danger of fire, and to prevent fire from spreading.

2 Water is the best means of putting out a fire, but water mains may be damaged in an air raid, or the flow restricted by fire fighting operations. So fill all spare buckets, cans, basins with water and keep them in readiness about the house in get-at-able places. Keep the bath full of water so that you can refill them.

3 Have a box of dry sand, or foamed slag, or earth, with a shovel fitted with a long handle, placed on an upper floor, for controlling an incendiary bomb. Better still, have a Redhill sand container with scoop—see page 32.

4 If you can manage it, coat all woodwork in the attic or roof space with limewash, to delay its catching fire. The mixture to be used is 2 lb. of slaked lime and 1 oz. of common salt with 1 pint of *cold* water. Apply 2 coats.

5 Get ready some simple fire fighting appliances if you have them or can get them ; see page 32. Also, if the materials are available, protect the floor of the loft, attic, or top floor in one of the following ways—with sheets of corrugated iron or plain sheet iron (gauge 22 or thicker) or asbestos wallboard, or with 2 inches of sand (if the floor will bear the weight), or foamed slag.

6 Find out exactly the emergency fire brigade arrangements in your neighbourhood—whether fire patrols have been established and where the nearest auxiliary fire station or fire post will be.

THINGS TO DO IN AN AIR RAID

This section describes the ACTION you would need to take during a war, as soon as you received warning of the actual approach of hostile aircraft. Only at such a time will the value of the previous sections become fully apparent.

The head of the house takes command, and because everyone in the household knows what to do and where to go, there is no indecision and no panic. Risk is reduced to a minimum. Appointed tasks are undertaken, appointed places " manned " without hesitation and without confusion.

Warning of a threat of an air raid will be given in towns by definite signals. It will not be possible to indicate by means of these signals whether gas bombs are expected. But local warnings will be given wherever possible, if gas has been dropped.

IF YOU LIVE IN A TOWN IMMEDIATELY ON HEARING THE WARNING AS HEAD OF THE HOUSEHOLD YOU SHOULD . . .

Personally supervise the following precautions—

1 Send every member of the household immediately to the refuge-room, making certain that each person has a respirator.

Pets should, if possible, have been sent away into the country at the first sign of danger. But if they are still in the house they should be taken into the refuge-room, otherwise they may come into contact with gas, or get splashed by it, and contaminate you. But it should be remembered that animals will help to use up the supply of air in the room. To be on the safe side, count two dogs or cats as one person in choosing the size of your refuge-room.

2 Make some other member of the family, previously appointed for the purpose, responsible for checking that all the articles needed for the refuge-room are properly in place (see lists on pages 10, 18 and 19), and that the room is properly sealed up against gas, the fire put out, and the chimney blocked up. The blanket over the door should be made damp.

3 Go all round the house, closing all doors and all windows, to reduce the amount of gas which can get into any part of the house.

4 After dark, see that no lights are left burning that may be visible from outside.

5 Extinguish all fires in grates. Fires cause currents of air which may draw in gas from outside. Do not put out these fires with water, as this will fill the house with irritant fumes. Smother them with earth or sand or salt.

6 If you have electric light you may use it, but all gas points that are burning should be turned off. It is better to turn off the gas at the meter, in case the pipes in the house got damaged and began to leak. Do not use gas light or paraffin lamps in the refuge-room, and if you use candles do not burn more at a time than is necessary, to avoid using up oxygen. If the passages to the refuge-room are very dark, you may light them with candles.

7 See that the bath is full of water, as a supply in case of fire. Also fill all available buckets, cans, and basins. Put them about the house where they can be reached easily.

This information is given to guide you. Your own common-sense will tell you of other things to do, according to the position of your refuge-room and the type of house you live in.

When these duties have been seen to, the head of the house or other responsible person should go to the refuge-room, and after making certain that EVERYONE IS THERE SHOULD CLOSE THE DOOR AND SEE THAT THE SEALING ARRANGEMENTS ARE EVERYWHERE INTACT.

If the house is a large one, it would be a good thing for someone to stay outside the refuge-room, on an upper floor or in a trench or dug-out outside, as a watcher in case an incendiary bomb falls on the house or on a neighbouring building. This is not necessary in small houses. The watcher should carry his respirator ready for instant use.

WHAT TO DO IN YOUR REFUGE-ROOM

These rules should be closely observed by all persons sheltering in a refuge-room.

1 Sit, or preferably lie down, and keep still, keeping warm with blankets or other coverings.

2 Don't smoke.

3 Don't light fires.

4 Don't go out, unless you must, until you hear the "Raiders passed" signal. Be very cautious even then. The danger of gas may not be over although the air raid may have ended. Only one member of the household should go out first to investigate, and he should be wearing his respirator.

5 Pass the time reading, writing, sewing, playing cards or quiet games, listening to the wireless or gramophone. Avoid exertion. Don't let the children romp about as they will only tire themselves out and get exhausted.

6 Do not put on your respirator unless the room is damaged, unless you have to go out, unless you actually smell gas. Remember, too, that a respirator affords no protection against ordinary coal gas.

7 Do not eat food that has come into contact with gas. That is why a food-chest of some kind, or air-tight jars and tins, are absolutely essential.

> *Don't forget, on coming out of your refuge-room, that whether the raid is over or not, you may find the rest of the house full of gas. So, except in emergency, keep your family in the refuge-room until you are sure the house is free of gas, or until it has been cleared.*

WHAT TO DO IF THE HOUSE IS DAMAGED

At once put on your respirator. If you have to go out of your refuge-room, seek refuge in another room or in another building.

If you have to go out of doors keep on your respirator, and wear a mackintosh and goloshes or gum boots if you have them. Walk with extreme care. Avoid all damp splashes on the ground that might be gas. Though the hostile aircraft may have gone there may be gas drifting about or splashed on the ground.

If anyone is injured, a message should be sent to the doctor or the nearest first aid party or post as quickly as possible. Until help comes you should treat an injured person according to the instructions in Section 5, at the end of the book.

HOW TO AVOID INJURY FROM MUSTARD GAS

Your respirator will completely protect your face, eyes, and lungs from mustard gas. But mustard gas can injure any part of the body with which it comes in contact.

Do not touch anything that may have been splashed with liquid gas. If you do, or think you may have done so, wash that part of yourself *immediately* with soap and water.

If you suspect that your clothing has come in contact with liquid gas, take off the outer garment *immediately*, and then as soon as possible take off the rest of your clothing and wash yourself with soap and water. Change your clothing also if you have passed through an area which has been splashed with liquid gas.

The contaminated clothing you have taken off should be thrown out of the house at once, until it can be decontaminated.

These are the best things to do if you can do them quickly. Then go to the nearest first aid post. But there is no need to go to a first aid post unless (1) you have been actually splashed with liquid gas or (2) you have passed through an area which has been splashed with liquid gas. In any case, take your own precautions first by washing and changing straight away.

WHAT TO DO IF FIRE BREAKS OUT

1 Do your best to put the fire out **yourself.**

2 If you cannot do so, summon help at once. Call a fire patrol or fire party, or inform a policeman or air raid warden. Have someone on the look-out so that, when the firemen arrive, they can get to work without delay.

3 See to the safety of all those in the house. If the refuge-room is in danger, get the occupants out. See that they have their respirators on and know what to do.

4 If the gas pipes in the house are damaged, turn the gas supply off at the main, if this has not been done already.

General guidance for dealing with fires

Any ordinary fire can be put out with water, which should be applied, with force, at the seat of the fire. A fire resulting from an incendiary or explosive bomb is like an ordinary fire. It is only the incendiary bomb itself which requires special treatment. This is described on the opposite page.

Keep in mind the following rules.

Close *all* doors and windows and keep them closed. If room doors are left open the staircase will act as a flue and the fire will quickly spread. A closed door will confine the fire for a time.

If you have to open a door which may have fire on the other side, and it opens towards you, place your foot a few inches from it before turning the handle. The door may fly open, but your foot will check it. The door will protect you against smoke, flame and hot gases, and you can shut it again if necessary. By keeping close to a wall, it is often possible to move quite safely about a room or a corridor or down a staircase which has been weakened by the effect of fire.

When you have to go near the seat of a fire, keep low and crawl if necessary, because the smoke and fumes are much less thick near the floor.

How to deal with an incendiary bomb

You can tackle a small incendiary bomb yourself (better if you have someone to help you) if you will follow these directions. You will also be able to get proper instruction about it.

The bomb will burn fiercely for a minute or so, throwing out burning sparks, and afterwards less fiercely. It will set fire to anything inflammable within reach. You should try to deal with it before it has caused a big fire.

Before you can get close enough to do anything, you will probably have to cool down the room with water, preferably with a line of hose. (See page 32 for a simple hand pump.)

After the preliminary use of the hose you should be able to get within 5 or 6 feet of the bomb and to place sand or other controlling material over it with a long-handled shovel. Use *dry* sand, or foamed slag, which is lighter, for controlling the bomb or, if you cannot get either, use dry sifted earth ; but it must be virgin soil from deep down, free from root fibres or vegetable matter.

About 35 lb. of sand (or earth) or 15 lb. of foamed slag should be sufficient to cover and control a small bomb. The best method of applying it is by the Redhill sand container and scoop (see page 32) ; but a bucket will do if you have a long-handled shovel to use with it.

When the bomb is under control, lift it in the scoop or on a shovel, place it in the sand container or bucket, and remove it out of doors as speedily as possible. Always keep about 2 or 3 inches of sand or earth or foamed slag in the bottom of the bucket to prevent the bomb burning through it.

When you have got rid of the bomb, tackle the fire with water. Under certain conditions the bomb may be controlled with a jet of water alone, without the use of sand.

ACT PROMPTLY. PROMPT ACTION MAY BE THE MEANS OF SAVING LIVES. PROMPT ACTION WILL SAVE PROPERTY. PROMPT ACTION WILL PREVENT SERIOUS DAMAGE. PROMPT ACTION WILL DEFEAT THE OBJECT OF THE RAID.

WHAT TO DO WHEN OUT OF DOORS

Always carry a respirator with you throughout the war

If you are out of doors at the time of an air raid, seek shelter at once. If it is impossible to get under cover it is safer to lie on the ground than to stand up, unless you stand in a doorway or narrow archway.

A limited number of public refuges will be available which will provide some protection for those caught in the streets.

Remember other people caught out of doors

If you have any space to spare in your refuge-room, and there is no special reason for not admitting strangers, be ready to take in someone who is caught in the street outside.

WHAT TO DO WHEN YOU COME OUT OF YOUR REFUGE-ROOM

Remember that gas may still be about after the " Raiders Passed " signal has been sounded.

If you detect gas in your house, keep your refuge-room closed up, but open all the other windows and doors. If you are in doubt, summon an air raid warden.

If you know bombs have fallen close by, go all round the house to see if any damage has been done. Look out of doors to see if your neighbours want any help.

If you have turned off the domestic gas supply at the main, inspect every gas point as soon as you turn it on again to make sure that no tap was left on or has been turned on accidentally.

Unexploded bombs

If you know of a bomb which has fallen but has not exploded, tell a policeman or air raid warden at once.

Leave it alone and keep away from it. It may still explode, even some time after it has been dropped. But this does not apply to a small incendiary bomb, which may be carefully picked up, if it is in a building or dangerous place, and carried in a bucket of water to a place of safety.

EXTRA PRECAUTIONS

This section describes extra precautions it is useful to take if you can, and refers to some inexpensive but effective fire fighting appliances. The extra precautions provide an additional protection against the effect of explosive bombs and against the penetration of gas. But do not be worried if they are more than you are able to take. The simpler precautions described in Section 2 are the essential things to do.

EXTRA PRECAUTIONS AGAINST EXPLOSIVE BOMBS

TRENCHES. Instead of having a refuge-room in your house, you can, if you have a garden, build a dug-out or a trench. A trench provides excellent protection against the effects of a bursting bomb, and is simple to construct; but keep it away from the house to avoid falling débris. The danger to beware of is the danger of gas. Although the risk of a heavy concentration of gas is not great, anyone using a trench or dug-out must, without fail, have his respirator with him. Precautions must also be taken against the risk of being splashed by liquid gas when out of doors. Overhead cover should be provided along at least part of the trench; a foot of earth spread over corrugated iron, or even boards, will do. The unprotected part should be dug a little deeper to keep the covered end dry. Do not try to make a trench in waterlogged ground.

SANDBAGS. Sandbags outside are the best protection if your walls are not thick enough to resist splinters. Do not rely on a wall keeping out splinters unless it is more than a foot thick.

A window opening protected by sandbags

The illustration on right shows side view

Sandbags are also the best protection for window openings. If you can completely close the window opening with a wall of sandbags (which should overlap the walls each side by about a foot) you will prevent the glass being broken by the blast of an explosion, as well as keeping out splinters. But the window must still be sealed inside against gas. A sandbag wall part of the way up a window will keep out splinters from the lower part of the room, but will not save the glass.

A wall of sandbags should be broader at the base than at the top. It should be in contact with the house-walls round the window opening.

Any bags or sacks, including paper sacks such as are used for cement, will do for sandbags. But if they are large, don't fill them right up or you won't be able to carry them. If you cannot get sand, use earth instead. It will serve as well.

If you haven't got sandbags, a wall of boxes filled with earth will do instead. The box wall should not be less than 2 ft. 6 ins. thick. If the boxes are large, fill them in position and ram the earth well down.

A basement window protected by boxes of earth

If your refuge-room is in a basement, and the window opens on to an area which you cannot fill in or cover over, build a wall of sandbags or boxes of earth round the top of the cellar area. See illustration above.

Save any small sacks or cloth bags or stout paper sacks you may get from time to time, even a few will be useful. Collect now wooden boxes or large cardboard cartons that will hold earth.

SIMPLE APPLIANCES FOR FIRE FIGHTING

Water is the best means of putting out fires, but its effect is much greater if it is applied through a jet with force behind it.

The simplest appliance for household use is the **Stirrup hand pump** (Home Office specification). It has 30 feet of hose, but no water container, and is used to pump water out of an ordinary bucket.

Sand for throwing on a fire cannot be easily scooped out of an ordinary round bucket with an ordinary shovel. The **Redhill sand container** (Home Office specification) is square-sided and has a suitably shaped scoop, with a long jointed handle. It is also strong enough to hold a small incendiary bomb without risk of the metal being burnt through.

If you cannot afford to buy both a hand pump and a Redhill sand container, the hand pump is the more important, because a sand container can be improvised.

EXTRA PRECAUTIONS AGAINST GAS

You have been told how to seal your refuge-room against gas. Try also to keep gas out of the rest of the house by blocking up ventilators, and cracks, as recommended for the refuge-room, and by protecting as many windows as possible against being broken by blast, as described on page 16. Then if you shut all windows and doors before a raid, there will be much less risk of gas penetrating into the house while you are in the refuge-room.

An additional precaution in flats or large buildings would be an air-lock at the door of a communal refuge-room, or at a main outer door, or in a corridor which had to be used frequently. An air-lock is simply two gas-proof doors or curtains 4 feet or more apart, with a space between them sealed like a refuge-room. Persons can then pass through without admitting gas, provided they close the first door or curtain when they are inside the air-lock before opening the second.

WHAT TO DO
IF ANYONE IS HURT

If you carry out the precautions given in this book you will know that you have done everything you reasonably can to protect yourself and those dependent on you. It is possible, however, that someone in your household might be injured. That is why those who can should learn something about first aid.

Some general principles are given here, but a simple first aid training —which may prove useful to anyone in everyday life—may be had from the St. John Ambulance Brigade, the St. Andrew's Ambulance Association, or the British Red Cross Society. You can get information about the training available in your own locality from your local Council Offices.

A list of simple first aid supplies is given on page 19.

ALL persons involved in accidents suffer from shock, whether or not they suffer physical injury. Shock is a disturbance of the nervous system. It varies in its severity. The signs of shock are faintness, paleness, weak pulse, and weak breathing.

TREATMENT OF SHOCK

1 Place the patient flat on his back on a bed or a rug or on cushions. If you think a bone may be broken do not move the patient more than can be helped.

2 Loosen the clothing at the neck, chest and waist to make the breathing freer.

3 Cover the patient warmly with rugs and blankets. In cases of shock the body loses heat. A hot-water bottle is helpful, but take care that it does not lie in contact with the skin.

4 Give hot drinks. If you cannot make hot drinks, give cold water *in sips*. But only if the patient is conscious and able to swallow.

5 Soothe the patient by speaking reassuring words in a calm voice and in a confident way.

TREATMENT OF WOUNDS

The first thing to do is to stop the bleeding and to keep the wound clean. This can be done by covering it with a clean dressing bound on tightly. Do not touch a wound with your fingers because of the risk of poisoning from dirt. Treat the patient for shock in addition to attending to the wound, because the loss of blood, if the wound is serious, and the pain do in themselves cause shock.

WOUNDS IN THE HEAD AND BODY

1 Cover the wound with a clean folded handkerchief or a double layer of dry lint.

2 Apply another handkerchief or a layer of cotton wool as a pad to distribute the pressure over the wound.

3 Tie the dressing firmly in position with a bandage, a strip of linen, or a necktie.

4 Treat the patient for shock.

WOUNDED LIMBS

1 First raise the limb to lessen the flow of blood.

2 If the flow of blood is steady (when a vein is injured) cover the wound with a dressing, and bandage it firmly as already described.

3 If the blood comes in spurts and the blood itself is brilliant red (when an artery is injured), raise the limb, and grasp it tightly between the wound and the point where the limb joins the body. Get someone else to apply dressings in the way already described. Keep the limb well raised. Release your grasp. Watch carefully. If the bleeding starts again, renew your grip and hold the limb firmly until skilled help arrives. If it is too tiring to keep your grasp, tie the limb firmly with a piece of stout string or a bandage, insert a stick (or a large skewer, or spoon, or fork) in the knot as shown in the illustration, and twist it until the bleeding stops. Then tie the stick, or whatever you use, firmly in position.

4 Treat the patient for shock.

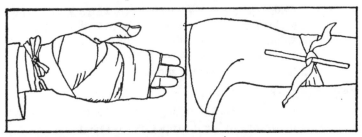

TREATMENT FOR BROKEN BONES

If bones or limbs are broken it is extremely unwise to move the patient more than is absolutely necessary. The patient often assumes by instinct a position in which the broken limb or bone is most comfortable. If you are doubtful whether a bone is broken, act as though it is, and do not move the patient unless you must.

1 Support the patient with cushions or folded blankets tucked closely around the body so that he can relax into the position he finds most comfortable.

2 A temporary arm-sling will sometimes relieve the pain of a broken arm.

3 A broken leg can sometimes be made more comfortable by being tied to the other leg at the thighs, calves and ankles by strips of linen or neckties.

4 Treat the patient for shock.

TREATMENT OF BURNS AND SCALDS

1 Cover the burned or scalded part with a *dry* dressing, a clean folded handkerchief, a pad of clean cotton wool, or a piece of lint folded double. Do *not* apply oil or butter to the burn.

2 Treat the patient for shock.

TREATMENT FOR GAS

Many of the gases which might be used in war are not necessarily dangerous to life if proper care is taken.

The first and most important thing is to keep calm.

Contaminated clothes should at once be taken off and thrown out. If any part of the body seems to be affected, wash it if possible. For example, the eyes should be freely washed out, the skin washed with soap and water, the throat and mouth gargled.

Until skilled assistance can be obtained, the patient should be kept as quiet as possible. He must not drink alcohol or smoke.

PLEASE think about what you have read and, so far as you can, act upon it. Decide *now* where your refuge-room ought to be. Think how you can make it as secure as possible. Start to collect the things you would need in it. Know what to do in case of fire. Learn how to deal with small incendiary bombs. Learn, too, a little about first aid. Make a point of knowing what is being done by your Local Authority in the way of air raid precautions, and understand how they affect you personally. If you want further advice, apply to your local Council Offices. If you feel able to volunteer for any air raid precautions work, offer your services to your local Council.

Other handbooks, described below, can be obtained from H.M. Stationery Office at the addresses given at the foot of the page, or through any bookseller.

A handbook on " Air Raid Precautions in Factories and Business Premises" (A.R.P. Handbook No. 6). Of interest to all employers. Price 6d. (7d. post free).

A handbook on " Personal Protection against Gas " (A.R.P. Handbook No. 1), which will interest all who want to know more about gas. Price 6d. (8d. post free).

A Home Office pamphlet, " Fire Protection : Hints to Householders," about fire risks in ordinary times. Price 3d. (3½d. post free).

Further information on protected accommodation is being prepared, and will be published later.

A.R.P. Handbooks may be purchased directly from H.M. STATIONERY OFFICE at the following addresses :

Adastral House, Kingsway, London, W.C.2
120 George Street, Edinburgh 2
26 York Street, Manchester 1
1 St. Andrew's Crescent, Cardiff
or through any bookseller

(456) Wt. 40580—282. 50M. 3/38. W. C. & S., Ltd. Gp. 389.

Air Raid Precautions
HANDBOOK No. 1

(2nd Edition)

PERSONAL PROTECTION
AGAINST GAS

LONDON
HIS MAJESTY'S STATIONERY OFFICE
Price 6d. net

AIR RAID PRECAUTIONS
HANDBOOK No. 1
(2nd Edition)

PERSONAL PROTECTION
AGAINST GAS

Issued by the Home Office
(Air Raid Precautions Department)

LONDON
PRINTED AND PUBLISHED BY HIS MAJESTY'S STATIONERY OFFICE

To be purchased directly from H.M. STATIONERY OFFICE at
the following addresses :
Adastral House, Kingsway, London, W.C.2 ; 120 George Street, Edinburgh 2
26 York Street, Manchester 1 ; 1 St. Andrew's Crescent, Cardiff ;
80 Chichester Street, Belfast ;
or through any bookseller

1938
Price 6*d.* net

List of Air Raid Precautions Handbooks

No. 1.—Personal Protection against Gas (*2nd edition*) price 6*d*. : 8*d*. post free.

A general handbook on gas dangers.

No. 2.—First Aid and Nursing for Gas Casualties (*3rd edition*) price 4*d*. : 5*d*. post free.

A handbook designed for nurses and for services giving first aid to air raid casualties.

No. 3.—Medical Treatment of Gas Casualties (*1st edition*) price 6*d*. : 8*d*. post free.

A handbook for hospitals and doctors.

No. 4.—Decontamination of Materials (*1st edition*) price 6*d*. : 7*d*. post free.

Decontamination of streets, buildings and their contents, vehicles and plant.

No. 5.—Structural precautions against Bombs and Gas (*in preparation*).

Structural protection against bombs and gas in buildings ; air raid shelters, either separate or in buildings. This handbook will be designed for use by architects, builders, and others directly responsible for the construction or maintenance of buildings.

No. 6.—Air Raid Precautions in Factories and Business Premises (*1st edition*) price 6*d*. : 7*d*. post free.

A handbook designed primarily for the guidance of occupiers of such premises.

No. 7.—Anti-Gas Precautions for Merchant Shipping (*2nd edition*) price 3*d*. : 3½*d*. post free.

Includes certain recommendations to Port Authorities.

In addition to these Handbooks, there is published a series of A.R.P. Memoranda dealing with various aspects of the organization to be provided by local authorities for public air raid precautions services (see list on back cover).

GENERAL PREFACE.

The series of Air Raid Precautions Handbooks (of which a list is given on the opposite page) is produced, under the authority of the Secretary of State, by the Air Raid Precautions Department of the Home Office with the assistance of other Government Departments concerned.

The measures for safeguarding the civil population against the effects of air attack which these Handbooks describe have become a necessary part of the defensive organisation of any country which is open to air attack. The need for them is not related to any belief that war is imminent. It arises from the fact that the risk of attack from the air, however remote it may be, is a risk that cannot be ignored, and because preparations to minimise the consequences of attack from the air cannot be improvised on the spur of the moment but must be made, if they are to be effective, in time of peace.

For the purpose of the measures now to be taken, it must be assumed that the scale of attack would greatly exceed anything which was experienced in the last war, and would involve the use of high explosive and incendiary bombs.

The use of poison gas in war is forbidden by the Geneva Gas Protocol of 1925, to which this country and all the most important countries of western Europe are parties, and the Government would use every endeavour on an outbreak of war to secure an undertaking from the enemy not to use poison gas. Nevertheless, the risk of poison gas being used remains a possibility and cannot be disregarded.

The Handbooks are designed to describe a scheme of precautions which it is hoped would prove effective in preventing avoidable injury and loss of life, or widespread dislocation of national activities. The Handbooks aim at giving the best available information on methods of passive defence against air attack, and will be revised from time to time in the light of future developments

CONTENTS

1st Edition, August, 1936. (477,000 copies.)
2nd Edition, March, 1938.

LIST OF ILLUSTRATIONS

GLOSSARY OF TECHNICAL TERMS.

Air-lock ... ... A compartment or lobby at the entrance to a gas protected building or room which enables persons to pass in and out without admitting gas.

Anti-Dim Outfit ... The materials provided for treating glass eyepieces of respirators so as to prevent dimming by moisture.

Bleaching Powder ... Chloride of lime.

Concentration ... The proportion of gas in a given volume of air.

Container ... ... The part of the respirator containing the charcoal to absorb true gases and the particulate to prevent the passage of finely divided particles of smokes, etc.

Contamination ... The liquid or vapour remaining on an object or person as a result of exposure to gas (usually a persistent gas).

Decontamination ... A process intended to remove the contaminating gas or to render it harmless. This word is not used to describe the cleansing of *persons*.

Facepiece ... ... The part of a respirator which covers the face.

Gas	Includes any chemical substance, solid, liquid or gas, used in war for its poisonous or irritant effects on the human body.
Non-persistent gas ...	A gas which forms a cloud (not necessarily visible) immediately it is released and leaves no liquid contamination on the ground.
Persistent gas	A gas in liquid form which evaporates slowly and so continues to give off dangerous vapour for a long period.
Respirator	An apparatus designed to protect the eyes and lungs from gas.

INTRODUCTION

Knowledge about personal protection against gas, both individual and collective, will be of vital importance to members of all air raid precautions services, and to every one whose duties might involve working or remaining in a gas concentration. The information contained in this handbook is intended to give not only rules of protection but also a general knowledge of the nature and dangers of war gases.

Individual protection, which consists in the wearing of a respirator and possibly anti-gas clothing, is fully described in this book.

Collective protection against gas consists in resort to a room or refuge which has been protected against the entry of gas. In this way the use of respirators and other methods of individual protection is rendered unnecessary so long as the gas-protection of the room or refuge remains undamaged. Collective protection is therefore to be regarded as the first line of defence for those not required to be out of doors on duty, and the respirator as the second line.

Methods of gas-protecting buildings are not dealt with in this book because they are closely **bound up** with protection against splinters and blast, and the whole subject is covered in other publications.

A short glossary of technical terms has been included at the beginning of this book, which the reader is advised to study before proceeding with the chapters which follow.

B

CHAPTER I

THE NATURE AND PROPERTIES OF WAR GASES

1. What is meant by " Gas "

By the term " gas " in warfare is meant any chemical substance, whether solid, liquid or vapour, which is used because it produces poisonous or irritant effects on the human body.

Such substances are generally liberated in the air as vapours or irritant smokes. They mix with the air and produce their harmful effects upon any unprotected persons who are exposed to this atmosphere. In the case of certain of the chemical substances, such as mustard gas, a serious effect is also caused by direct contact of the human body with the liquid itself or with objects which have become contaminated by the liquid.

For convenience it is usual to divide gases into two main groups:—

    (*a*) Non-persistent.
    (*b*) Persistent.

When liberated into the air, " non-persistent " gases form clouds of gas or smoke which drift along with the wind, gradually mixing with larger quantities of air and so becoming less dangerous. Examples of such substances are chlorine, phosgene and the irritant smokes produced from certain compounds of arsenic.

" Persistent gases " are usually liquids which evaporate slowly, giving off dangerous vapour. The ground and any other object on which the liquid has fallen will continue to give off vapour until the liquid has all evaporated, or until steps have been taken to render it ineffective.

In the case of mustard gas or other blister gases, contact with the contaminated ground or objects will give rise to skin burns until decontamination has been effected. Even walking over contaminated ground is dangerous and must be avoided.

Mustard gas and many of the tear gases are examples of this persistent class.

In an air raid, the essential difference between the " non-persistent " gases and the " persistent " gases would be that a bomb containing the former would produce a cloud of gas which would be carried away by the wind, whereas a bomb containing the latter would spatter liquid around the point of burst, and the affected ground would require special treatment (" decontamination ") to render it safe.

2. Effect of Weather

The effectiveness of a " gas " may be considerably influenced by the weather. A high wind rapidly blows away non-persistent gas or vapour arising from an area contaminated by persistent gas, but it does not remove the danger which results from touching objects or ground contaminated by the latter.

In warm weather, persistent liquids will give off vapour which will rise and readily become mixed with the surrounding air, but on the other hand the liquid will evaporate more quickly than in cold weather. Consequently, under warm weather conditions the danger from vapour will be greater. Frosty weather has little effect upon the clouds of non-persistent gases, but liquids such as mustard gas may freeze under cold conditions. In the frozen state, direct contact will still produce skin burns, but there is less danger from vapour. When it thaws, the liquid will again begin to give off vapour.

Light rain has little effect upon gases of either class, but heavy rain tends to wash gas out of the air and also helps to wash away and destroy any liquid upon the ground. The most dangerous conditions under which any gas may be used are in mild calm weather, with cr without fog. The absence of wind means that the rate of mixing of the gas with air will be slow, and therefore the gas will drift about in dangerous concentrations for a long time. Under these conditions gas may slowly penetrate into buildings through small inlets which have been overlooked.

3. Effects produced by Gas on Personnel

The division of gases into two main groups—non-persistent and persistent—is convenient because, as soon as the class of a gas has been determined, it is possible to decide whether or not the area in which the gas has been liberated requires special treatment. In addition they may be classified according to the effects which they produce upon the human body. These groups are designated by the following names:—

    (*a*) Tear gas.
    (*b*) Nose irritant gas.
    (*c*) Lung irritant gas.
    (*d*) Blister gas.

(a) *Tear gas*.—Any eye irritant which even in very small amounts has an immediate effect upon the eyes, causing intense smarting, a profuse flow of tears and spasm of the eyelids, which generally make it very difficult to see. In pure air the effects of the vapour soon pass off, and no damage is caused to the eyes though the *liquid* of a persistent tear gas *may* cause permanent injury to the eye.

These gases are often called " lachrymators."

(b; *Nose irritant gas*.—Irritant smokes produced from certain arsenical compounds are in this class, but though they produce intense pain in the nose, throat and breathing passages during exposure to the gas, these painful effects soon pass off in fresh air.

(c) *Lung irritant gas.*—An irritant gas which attacks the breathing passages and lungs. Chlorine and phosgene are examples of this type, and will produce death if breathed in sufficiently large quantities.

These gases are sometimes called " choking gases."

(d) *Blister gases.*—These substances, of which mustard gas is a typical example, cause intense irritation or burning of the skin according to the amount of gas which has come into contact with the affected part. In severe cases deep and extensive blisters may be caused.

These gases are also known as " vesicants."

No immediate pain is felt on contact with mustard gas in the solid, liquid or vapour form, but the effects become apparent a few hours later.

Mustard gas also attacks the eyes and lungs, but in these cases also there is considerable delay before the symptoms are noticed, and it is this absence of immediate effect which constitutes one of the greatest dangers of mustard gas. The need for protection is not appreciated until too late.

The effects produced by any war gas depend on the amount of the gas and the length of time a person is exposed to it. The stronger the gas, the greater will be the injury produced in a given time. It should not, however, be assumed that small quantities of gas will always cause injury. In the case of gases which injure the lungs, a certain quantity must be breathed before it will do any real harm. A person working hard is breathing a much greater volume of air than a person sitting still, so that, if both were exposed to the same concentration of gas, the person working hard would suffer the greater injury. Only under exceptional conditions is there likely to be sufficient gas present in the air to render one or two breaths dangerous.

4. Types of the more important Gases

The methods by which these gases may be detected are more fully described in Chapter III.

(a) TEAR GASES

(*i*) **Chlor-aceto-phenone (C.A.P.)** (*Non-persistent*).— This substance is a white crystalline solid which vaporizes when heated. The cloud so produced is intensely tear-producing. In high concentrations the gas has an irritating effect upon the exposed skin.

(*ii*) **Ethyl-iodo-acetate (K.S.K.)** (*Persistent*).—This compound when pure is a colourless oily liquid with a pungent smell like peardrops. The liquid as used however is generally dark in colour. It evaporates slowly at ordinary temperatures; when spattered upon the ground the lachrymatory effects of the vapour persist for some hours.

It is a strong tear gas, and in high concentrations a respiratory irritant.

(*iii*) **Bromo-benzyl-cyanide (B.B.C.)** (*Persistent*).— This substance as generally used is a brown liquid with a very penetrating smell. The effect of the vapour on the eyes is not quite as intense as that of the previous compound, but the liquid is much more persistent. Under suitable weather conditions the lachrymatory effect may be noticed several days after contamination with this liquid.

(b) NOSE IRRITANT GASES

Di-phenyl-chlor-arsine (D.A.) *and similar compounds, such as* **di-phenyl-amine-chlor-arsine (D.M.)** *and* **di-phenyl-cyano-arsine (D.C.)** (*Non-persistent*).—These arsenical substances can be liberated into the air as smokes, which, like tobacco smoke, really consist of very minute particles rather than actual gas or vapour. Quite small quantities of the " gas," which are invisible to the eye, will produce intense irritation and pain in the nose and throat, which are often accompanied by sneezing. The first effect noticed is irritation of the nose and throat. This is followed by a burning sensation in the chest, headache, and aching in the teeth and gums. These effects may not subside, and may seem to increase, on first removal into pure air, or on putting on the respirator; but they are nevertheless of a temporary nature and no permanent injury results.

High concentrations of these gases produce irritation of the eyes, in addition to the previously mentioned symptoms in more severe form.

(c) LUNG IRRITANT GASES

(*i*) **Chlorine** (*Non-persistent*).—This substance has an unpleasant suffocating smell, and, when undiluted, has a greenish yellow colour. It is readily liquefied at ordinary temperatures, by the application of pressure, and is therefore usually stored in steel cylinders. It attacks most metals and is soluble in water.

Chlorine is a powerful irritant of the respiratory organs. Exposure to the gas causes a burning sensation in the eyes, nose and throat, which may be followed by waterlogging of the lungs. Prolonged breathing of high concentrations of the gas will cause death.

(*ii*) **Phosgene** (*Non-persistent*).—This compound is a colourless gas at ordinary temperatures, though when liberated as a cloud it sometimes has a whitish appearance owing to condensation of water vapour present in the air. At low temperatures it forms a colourless liquid, and is stored in this form. It has a pungent odour rather like musty hay and is liable to cause coughing. In addition to being a very powerful lung irritant, phosgene is also a tear gas. It attacks the air cells of the lungs which, in severe cases, gradually become filled with inflammatory fluid resulting in interference with the passage of oxygen into the blood.

In this state exertion will cause the patient to collapse from want of oxygen, and death is then frequently the result.

There is frequently a period of "well being" between the initial effects caused by exposure to phosgene and the appearance of the more serious symptoms. This is the meaning of the so-called "delayed action" of phosgene.

(d) BLISTER GASES

(*i*) **Mustard gas** (ββ'—*di-chloro-di-ethyl sulphide*) (*Persistent*).—This substance is an oily liquid, probably dark brown in colour, with a faint but characteristic smell. Some people consider this smell like mustard, others associate it with horseradish, onions, or garlic. Some persons cannot detect the smell except in high concentrations.

It is readily soluble in certain liquids such as oils, benzene and methylated spirits, and also in tar and fat. Owing to its solubility in fat, it is quickly absorbed by the skin with subsequent injurious results. Similarly it is readily absorbed in the tar surface of roads.

It evaporates slowly at ordinary temperatures and is very persistent. It is a powerful irritant, and this effect can be caused by either the vapour or the liquid. Naturally the liquid is more effective than the vapour when brought in contact with the body.

Mustard gas differs from the gases previously dealt with since it may be dangerous in a number of ways. The principal sources of danger are given below:—

(i) When the ground or other objects have been splashed with liquid mustard, vapour is given off which may injure the eyes, the lungs or exposed parts of the body.

(ii) The vapour may also be absorbed by clothing and gradually penetrate to the skin, causing burns even after the wearer has moved out of the dangerous area.

(iii) If the contaminated ground or splashed objects are touched with the hand or other parts of the body, burns will be caused, unless immediate precautions are taken. Again, if the clothing rubs against anything which is contaminated, the liquid will be soaked up and the clothing may produce blisters. It also has to be remembered that whenever a person has become contaminated he is a source of danger to everyone with whom he comes into contact. If he gets mustard gas on his boots and goes into a room containing a number of other people, they may all be seriously affected by the vapour coming from the boots. Danger arises from the fact that the only means of appreciating the presence of mustard gas vapour is by the sense of smell and that the smell of the gas may easily pass unnoticed or be confused with other smells.

(iv) Persons may become contaminated by drops of mustard gas which have been released from aircraft in the form of a spray.

Neither the liquid nor the vapour produces any immediate recognizable sensation or effect. The symptoms do not become apparent for from two to eight hours afterwards, by which time it is too late to prevent injury. If a person is known to have been exposed to mustard gas vapour or contaminated by liquid and steps are taken to apply preventive measures quickly, injury may be avoided or at any rate much reduced.

The eyes are the part of the body most liable to be affected by mustard gas. To remain unprotected in an atmosphere containing even a small amount of mustard gas vapour for an hour will cause acute inflammation of the eyes. If more mustard gas is present a much shorter exposure will be injurious. Mustard gas vapour will also affect the respiratory system. Bronchitis or worse injury may result according to the quantity of mustard gas present and the time of exposure.

Both the vapour and the liquid will cause burns of the skin. An hour's exposure to even a small quantity of vapour will produce, after the usual delay period, a reddening and scalding of the exposed parts of the body, while high concentrations of vapour will produce blisters.

Serious damage may also result from the continued wearing of clothing which has been exposed to mustard gas vapour.

The effects of the liquid on the body are, of course, far more severe than those of the vapour. Liquid contamination of the skin must be treated at once.

(*ii*) **Lewisite** (β—*chloro-vinyl-di-chlor-arsine*) (*Persistent*).—This gas differs from mustard gas in that—

(*a*) it contains arsenic,

(*b*) it has a strong smell like that of geraniums,

(*c*) it is noticed at once owing to irritation of the eyes and nose, and

(*d*) it acts more rapidly than mustard gas.

Otherwise its characteristics and effects are generally similar to those of mustard gas.

CHAPTER II

THE METHODS OF GAS ATTACK FROM THE AIR

5. Bombs from Aircraft

Air bombs are particularly suitable for charging with gas because they do not have to withstand the shock of discharge from a gun, and can therefore have a much thinner steel casing than that of a shell. The quantity of gas which a bomb will hold is somewhere about half of the total weight of the bomb. In the case of a shell it is proportionately very much less.

The type of bomb used for the discharge of gas is a particularly effective weapon for the purpose because it does not bury itself deeply in the ground. Most of the gas is thus liberated on the surface, and the full effect is produced without being smothered.

Air bombs containing gas may be small or large, but the effects produced will be similar. In the case of a non-persistent gas the whole contents of the bomb will form a cloud near the point at which it strikes the ground and this cloud will drift along with the wind. The size of the cloud when first formed will be small, but the concentration of gas in it will be very great. As the cloud is swept along by the wind it will become diluted with more air, but its size will increase. After travelling a considerable distance the gas will become mixed with so much air that it will be harmless. The rate at which this process of dilution goes on will depend upon the weather conditions, particularly the strength of the wind.

In a high wind the cloud will be rapidly broken up, though gas may be forced into unexpected places by the wind pressure while the concentration is still high.

It is possible that a house which would resist the penetration of gas in calm weather might let in an appreciable quantity of gas in a strong wind. Generally speaking, however, the danger to be anticipated from a non-persistent gas will be very much reduced by high wind.

If there should be no wind at all, or only a slight drift, the worst situation will arise, though the effects will be more local. A dense cloud of gas will form at the point of burst and will remain in that particular area until it is gradually dispersed. It will find its way by diffusion and ventilation currents into areas, cellars, tunnels, etc., and once there it is not so readily cleared as the gas in the open streets. Once the gas has penetrated into a confined space it is not subject to the influence of the wind and air currents prevailing outside, and may continue to be dangerous when the outside air has become clear of gas.

It is possible that the nose irritant gases may be produced from some form of generator contained in a bomb. In this case the cloud will be emitted (for some minutes) from the place at which the bomb has fallen and the distance to which the gas will travel in an effective concentration may be considerably greater than with the other non-persistent gases.

A bomb containing persistent gas such as mustard gas will make a large splash of liquid at the place where the bomb dropped and will also cover a considerable area with fine droplets. The degree of contamination and the size of the area affected are dependent upon the size and type of the bomb, the nature of the ground on which it falls, and the strength of the wind. In hard ground penetration will be slight, and the liquid will be more widely distributed over the surrounding area. Again, if the wind is fairly strong, the drops formed by the shattering of the bomb may be carried down-wind for a considerable distance.

Anyone who is near the place where the bomb falls may be contaminated by the liquid drops or splashes and immediate action, as described in Chapter VI, must be taken to avoid serious injury.

Persons walking over gas-contaminated ground will be liable to contaminate their boots by stepping in liquid or picking up mud containing mustard gas. This danger will persist for a long period (usually some days), unless the area is decontaminated, and during this time the area must be railed off and all movement over it prevented.

A dangerous concentration of mustard gas vapour may also travel down-wind in exactly the same way as a cloud of non-persistent gas, though it will not usually be effective for the same distance. Unless the weather is very cold, the contaminated area will continue to give off vapour until it has been decontaminated and the recognised warning sign must be erected to warn persons of the danger from the vapour.

A bomb filled with tear gas will splash the ground in the same way as one filled with mustard gas. Evaporation of the liquid on the ground will produce a cloud of tear gas which will render a large area intolerable to persons who have no protection for their eyes. This vapour effect will continue for a number of days, or until the area is properly decontaminated.

The chief difference between the use of large and small bombs is that, for the same load, there will be in one case a few well-marked and heavily contaminated areas, and in the other case a large number of centres of contamination which might be more difficult to locate and clear.

6. Spray from Aircraft

Mustard gas or other persistent gas can be sprayed from aircraft. The liquid falls in fine drops over a fairly wide area. The drops may indeed be so small as not to be noticed by persons upon whom they may fall. Such a spray may be a source of very great danger, because it may fall on the face, neck, and any exposed parts of the body, in addition to the clothing, without being noticed.

Attention has been drawn to this method of releasing gas, and to the particular difficulties and risks which its use might cause, but its effectiveness must not be exaggerated. The risk to persons in the open will be obvious, but the danger may be avoided by remaining under cover.

Probably the greatest risk is from the use of a persistent gas such as mustard gas in conjunction with high explosive bombs. Material damage will be produced by the high explosive; and the mustard gas, whether used as spray or in bombs, will render the task of rescuing and treating casualties more difficult and hazardous.

CHAPTER III

THE DETECTION OF GASES

7. Principles of Gas Detection

The rapid transmission of information that gas has been used, with its nature and details of the areas affected, is a very necessary factor of success in air raid precautionary measures.

By gas detection is meant the recognition of the presence of gas and the identification of its type.

The presence of gas may be detected in a number of ways:—

    (i) by the smell,
   (ii) by immediate irritant effects,
  (iii) by visible signs,
  (iv) by chemical testing.

Most gases hitherto used in warfare have either a distinctive smell or a characteristic irritant effect on the eyes, nose or throat. In many cases also there will be visible indications of gas, such as the presence of a cloud or liquid splashes on the ground.

To a large extent, therefore, reliance can be placed upon the senses, particularly the sense of smell, but chemical tests may be available in addition for the identification of particular gases.

8. Detection of the various Types of Gas

Detection of tear gases

Tear gases are easily detected owing to their immediate irritant effect upon the eyes. As many of the tear gases are persistent, and consist of dark brown liquids, care must be taken not to confuse gases of this group with blister gas contamination.

Detection of nose irritant gases

Nose irritant gases are practically odourless. The first indication of their presence is likely to be irritation of the nose and throat, sneezing, etc. These gases are non-persistent.

Detection of lung irritant gases

Lung irritant gases are not difficult to detect as they all have a very characteristic odour. · The most important example of these gases, and the one most likely to be encountered, is phosgene. This gas has a pronounced smell of musty hay. At the time this smell is detected, irritation of the breathing passages with possibly some watering of the eyes may be noticed, but should not be waited for. Phosgene forms a thin white cloud when the atmosphere is moist, otherwise it is colourless. It is non-persistent.

Detection of blister gas

(i) Mustard Gas.—The odour of this substance is not powerful, nor are the effects immediate, and consequently persons are likely to under-estimate the danger. Mustard gas, whilst the most difficult gas to detect, can nevertheless be recognized in several ways, namely:—

      (*a*) by smell,
      (*b*) by visible signs,
      (*c*) by chemical testing.

The substance has a faint but characteristic smell suggestive of horseradish, onions, or garlic, but some people cannot smell it except in high concentrations. The presence of mustard gas vapour can readily be detected by a person familiar with its smell provided it is not masked by other odours, but after a short time the sense of smell becomes dulled and low concentrations of the gas may not be detected.

The liquid varies in colour from dark brown to pale straw colour. The gas given off from the liquid is invisible. The liquid, if of the pale colour, is difficult to detect on grass, trees, etc.; and it appears as a wet patch on dry roads or dry earth. On wet roads or earth it gives a slight iridescent effect, similar to that of paraffin on a wet surface. Detection of the liquid is not easy, but provided the smell is known the presence of the gas should be readily recognized.

(ii) *Lewisite.*—This substance differs from mustard gas in having a strong smell, like that of geraniums, and it is noticed at once owing to the irritation caused to the eyes and nose. Detection of lewisite should not therefore be difficult.

9. Chemical Indicators

Indicators have been devised which will assist in the identification of *liquid* blister gas and the subsequent defining of the contaminated area. The basis of these detectors consists of a special greenish yellow paint which shows a red discolouration on contact with *liquid* blister gas. It is important to note that the vapour of blister gas does not give any indication on the paint. These detectors consist of two kinds:—

(i) *Detectors, Spray.*—These are indicators painted with detector paint. These should be not less than about 18 inches square. Their purpose is to indicate rapidly the arrival of aircraft spray.

(ii) *Detectors, Ground.*—These consist of material painted with detector paint which, when brought into contact with a suspected contaminated surface, will give an indication if free liquid blister gas is present.

It should be noted that certain liquid tear gases, such as K.S.K. and B.B.C., also produce a reddish discolouration similar to that resulting from blister gas. These tear gases may be present when efforts are being made to detect blister gas, but they can be readily recognised by their powerful effect on the

c

eyes. When, therefore, tear gas is present it must be remembered that any colour change produced in the detector paint is not a certain indication of the presence or absence of blister gas. Similarly, when the presence of tear gas is indicated by smell, it must not be assumed that a red discolouration is due to the tear gas only, since blister gas may have been used in addition and the strong smell of the tear gas may be masking its presence.

The detection of the red colouration of the paint may also be rendered difficult by mud, or even, by the brown liquid of mustard gas itself.

In view of this limitation, any indications given by these detectors should be considered in conjunction with other observations made on the lines described in the preceding Sections.

CHAPTER IV

GENERAL ANTI-GAS PRECAUTIONS AND COLLECTIVE PROTECTION

10. How to avoid becoming a Casualty

The risk of injury by gas will be reduced to a minimum by observance of the following rules:—

(i) Immediately on hearing an air raid warning, take cover in a gas-protected room or refuge, unless your public duty compels you to go out of doors or remain at work in an unprotected place.

(ii) Have your respirator always with you.

(iii) Do not come out of the room or refuge without cautiously trying to discover whether gas is about. The local gas warning will give indication of definite danger.

(iv) If your duty prevents your taking cover during a raid, always have your respirator ready to put on at once, and your protective clothing if necessary.

The air raid warning will mean that a raid may occur in a few minutes (perhaps 5 to 7 minutes). When the raiding aircraft are reported clear of the district, a further message, " Raiders Passed ", will be issued. It must be realised that this message means simply that the raiders are no longer overhead : if they have dropped gas, the danger from the gas may remain, and those who leave cover on hearing the " Raiders Passed " signal must still take precautions against the possible presence of gas.

If after a raid there is any gas in the streets, the general public should so far as possible remain under cover until the area is reported clear; that is, until the gas has dissipated or the proper steps have been taken to neutralise it.

It should be remembered that outside walls, door-posts, lamp-posts and similar objects may be contaminated after a raid in which blister gas has been used, and care should therefore be taken not to touch or lean against them until they have been decontaminated.

Leather boots may be a source of danger, and are quite unsuitable for use in heavily contaminated places. When leather boots have unavoidably to be used in contaminated localities, they should first be thoroughly greased with a mixture of equal parts of bleaching powder and white petroleum jelly, such as vaseline just before being worn. This mixture will help to delay the penetration of blister gas into the leather, and should be wiped off when the boots are taken off before coming indoors. A fresh application should be made each time the boots are worn. To obtain the maximum protection with leather boots, only those with sound and thick soles should be used.

With due care and observance of instructions it is considered that most people should be able to avoid getting their boots contaminated.

Walking along a pavement or metalled road contaminated with blister gas will not cause serious contamination of the boots unless splashes or pools of liquid are lying about.

Persons who have walked through contaminated areas should examine the soles and uppers of their boots to make sure that the boots are not contaminated with liquid blister gas, taking care while doing so that they do not contaminate their hands. If any trace of blister gas can be seen or smelt the boots must not be worn, and must be left out of doors until decontaminated (see Section 27).

11. Precautions for those out of doors in a gas-contaminated Area

The duties of members of air raid precautions services may necessitate their going into streets and through areas in which dangerous concentrations of gas exist.

Contaminated areas or streets in which gas is present should be avoided if possible, and where duty makes it essential to approach a gassed area every care should be taken to avoid unnecessary contamination. Thus, it is important to keep to windward of bomb craters, and to avoid stepping on earth or débris which has been scattered about the streets, and which may be contaminated.

Whenever the presence of gas can be detected by the sense of smell, or by the effect on the eyes or throat, and whenever it is necessary to pass downwind of craters which have been marked as dangerous from gas, the respirator must always be worn. It must not be removed until the wearer has tested the air, by inserting the fingers between the facepiece and the cheek and sniffing gently. (This must not however be done if contaminated gloves are being worn).

If these simple but fundamental precautions are observed, the efficiency of each individual will be maintained and the number of gas casualties reduced to a minimum. Any person who becomes contaminated through carelessness is temporarily unable to fulfil his duties, and at the same time is putting an unnecessary strain upon the first aid services.

Careful training in anti-gas precautions will enable a person readily to appreciate when and where danger exists, and the steps to be taken to prevent his becoming a casualty.

12. Collective Protection in Buildings

Gas-protected accommodation should be regarded as the primary protection against gas for those whose duty does not compel them to be out of doors or to remain in an exposed place. This may take the form of a refuge-room at home or at their place of business, or a shelter or public refuge, depending on where they are. It is therefore an integral part of anti-gas training to know how to protect a room or shelter against gas. In ordinary buildings this can be done comparatively simply.

Methods of gas protection are described in the handbook " The Protection of Your Home against Air Raids," and in A.R.P. Handbook No. 6 " Air Raid Precautions in Factories and Business Premises," the relevant parts of which should be consulted by those concerned with anti-gas training.

Collective protection in gas-protected accommodation is a first line of defence against gas, but those provided with respirators should also have them at hand in case the gas protection is damaged. The design and use of respirators is described in the next Chapter

CHAPTER V

PROTECTION OF THE EYES AND LUNGS

The respirators which are described in this Chapter have all been designed to give protection against all types of gas which are likely to be used as war gases. The protection which they give against these gases is fully satisfactory, but it must be emphasized that they are not intended to afford protection against other gases which may be encountered in industrial processes or in everyday life. They do not, for example, protect against carbon monoxide which is present in coal gas, exhaust gases from motor cars and gases from sewers or drains, nor from petrol vapour in confined spaces, ammonia or similar toxic and noxious gases and vapours. These respirators should not therefore be relied upon for protection in the presence of peacetime dangers. In any event, they will not render the wearer safe in situations where the danger arises from a deficiency of oxygen.

Care must always be taken not to damage respirators by careless handling, or their efficacy may be inpaired. The instructions for their use and care must always be carefully observed.

13. The Civilian Respirator

The Civilian respirator must be described first, because it is the respirator intended for use by members of the general public, and a knowledge of it is required by everyone. Even those whose duties would require them to wear the Civilian Duty or Service respirator when at work must remember that they themselves when off duty, and their families in any case, would have to wear the Civilian respirator.

The Civilian respirator protects the wearer against breathing any of the known war gases and is to be used on occasions when gas is present and a gas-protected room or refuge is not available or has to be evacuated.

This respirator (*see* Fig. 1) consists essentially of : —

(i) a container filled with material to filter or absorb gas; and

(ii) a facepiece to cover the eyes, nose and mouth.

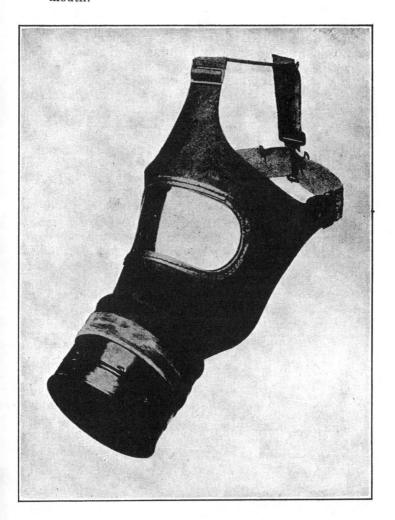

Fig. 1—Civilian Respirator.

The facepiece is made of rubber sheet, with a large window of non-inflammable transparent material. (This material might be damaged by the chemicals in many types of disinfectants and, as is mentioned in Appendix D, even the disinfectants approved for use with other respirators should not be used on the Civilian respirator.) The cylindrical container is securely attached to the facepiece by means of a strong rubber band. All the air breathed by the wearer passes through this container, which removes the poisonous gas.

No haversack is provided with this respirator, but it is issued in a stout cardboard carton which should be kept to preserve the respirator from damage.

The respirator covers the entire face and is held in position by means of three straps attached to the facepiece which meet in a buckle at the back of the head. By suitably adjusting the length of the straps a respirator of the appropriate size can be made to fit comfortably on any head. A safety pin is provided in the end of each strap so that when once the straps have been adjusted to the correct length they can be made secure against unintentional alteration by pinning the ends to the body of the straps.

When the respirator is worn the air drawn in through the container passes into the facepiece through a simple one-way valve attached to the inner end of the container. This valve closes on breathing out, thus preventing air being passed back through the container, and the pressure of the breath then lifts the edge of the facepiece very slightly away from the face at the cheeks and allows the breath to escape.

The respirator is made in three sizes. The difference between the sizes lies only in the size of the facepiece: the same container is fitted to each size.

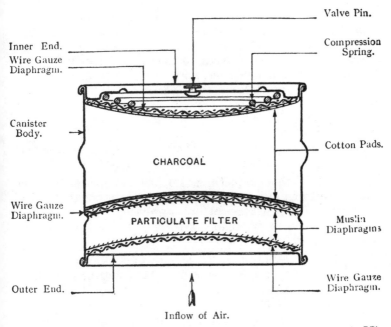

Valve Pin.

Compression Spring.

Inner End.

Wire Gauze Diaphragm.

Canister Body.

CHARCOAL

Cotton Pads.

Wire Gauze Diaphragm.

PARTICULATE FILTER

Muslin Diaphragms

Outer End.

Wire Gauze Diaphragm.

Inflow of Air.

FIG. 2—CIVILIAN RESPIRATOR CONTAINER (G.C. Mark II).

The container (known as G.C. Mark II—*see* Fig. 2) consists of a cylindrical tin canister (lacquered black) containing activated charcoal to absorb gases such as phosgene and mustard gas, and a particulate filter which prevents the passage of finely divided smokes like the arsenical gases. The contents of the container do not deteriorate either with age or with wearing the respirator when gas is not present. When used in gas the contents of the container slowly become exhausted, the rate of exhaustion depending upon the concentration of the gas and the length of time of wearing in gas, but the nature and amounts of the contents are such that the container will remain efficient for a very long time under the conditions in which it will be used by the general public.

When the respirator is issued for use in time of emergency it must first be fitted to the face of the person who is to wear it. It will then become the personal property of that person and it will be his or her duty to become familiar with the proper method of wearing and taking care of it.

Dimming

In order to prevent the eyepiece misting over when the respirator is worn, treat it as follows:—

(i) If the eyepiece is smeary or opaque as the result of previous wearing, sponge the inside lightly with clean water before applying the treatment described in (ii) below.

(ii) Wet the end of a finger and rub it on a piece of toilet soap. Then rub the finger all over the inside of the eyepiece so that a thin even film of soap covers the surface. The respirator is then ready to wear.

Use *toilet* soap only for this treatment.

(iii) Treat the eyepiece as described above when the respirator is removed, so that it will be ready for immediate use again. If the respirator is not worn, the soap film will remain effective for about one week.

(iv) If the film of soap is rubbed or scratched its efficiency will be impaired, so in order to obtain the best possible vision it is advisable whenever possible to treat the eyepiece immediately before use.

The Civilian respirator being worn is illustrated in Figure 3. Instructions as to its fitting and use are contained in Appendix A.

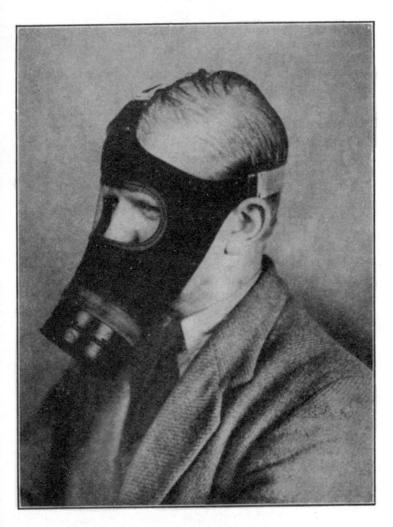

Fig. 3—Civilian Respirator being worn.

14. The Care of the Civilian Respirator

The respirator has been designed to withstand for a long time the wear due to ordinary use. Reasonable precautions must, however, be taken to preserve it in good and safe condition. The respirator should be regarded as a personal article upon which the wearer's safety may at some time depend, and it should be treated with the care to which such a safeguard is entitled. Apart from considerations of personal safety, economy of respirators would be most important in war, and it is particularly desirable that the many respirators which would never have to be used in gas should not have to be replaced on account of accidental or careless damage.

Careful attention to the proper method of putting on and removing the respirator will very greatly help in preserving it from damage. The wearer should take steps to become familiar with these operations and with wearing the respirator so that in an emergency, when haste may be necessary, damage to the respirator is not likely to be caused through ignorance or lack of practice in using it.

When not in use the respirator should be kept in a cool place away from strong light. Exposure to heat or prolonged exposure to strong light will cause deterioration of the materials from which the respirator is constructed and must be avoided. For instance, the respirator must not be dried before a fire or kept near a radiator or left standing on a window ledge.

If wet with rain the respirator should be dried with a soft cloth before being put away, taking care not to scratch or crease the transparent window.

After use the respirator will be wet on the inside with moisture from the breath. This moisture should be wiped out with a soft cloth and the inside of the respirator allowed to dry before it is put away.

Fig. 4.—Civilian Respirator Carton, Showing
Recess for Container.

Fig. 5.—Civilian Respirator Correctly Packed
in Carton.

The respirator should not be carried or hung suspended from the straps, for this would tend to weaken the rubber and might prevent the respirator fitting properly when it is next put on. When not actually in use it should always be kept and carried in the cardboard carton provided (*see* Fig. 4). It should be inserted with the container standing upright in the recess at the bottom of the carton, the facepiece being laid over *so that the transparent eyepiece lies evenly on the top of the container at full length, without any deformation* (*see* Fig. 5).

Care must be taken at all times to avoid damage to the transparent window. It must not be allowed to become creased, folded, scratched, or dented, or unnecessarily exposed to heat.

In order to maintain the respirator in a wholesome condition the inside of the facepiece and the top of the container may be sponged carefully with a sponge or soft cloth which has been dipped in luke-warm soapy water and squeezed free from excessive liquid. Only soap of toilet quality is to be used for this purpose and the water must not be hot. The soap must then be removed by sponging with clean water. When sponging the eyepiece, it must be supported on the outside with the palm of the hand. Care must be taken not to use an excessive amount of liquid, and no liquid must be allowed to enter the container or to remain between the rim of the container and the facepiece.

As to the disinfection of the Civilian respirator, see Appendix D. For its decontamination, see Section 28.

15. Inspection of Civilian Respirators

The following points should be included in the inspection of Civilian respirators.

(a) *Facepiece*

1. The rubber facepiece must not be perished, torn or punctured. The rubber is in serviceable condition

if it does not tear when a portion of the edge is gripped between the fingers and thumbs, with their tips about 1 inch apart, and stretched to a length of about 2 inches. Punctures can be detected by holding the facepiece up to the light and stretching the rubber gently.

2. The stitching by which the tapes are attached to the facepiece must be sound and the attachment secure.

3. The transparent window must not be torn, punctured or split and the stitching around its edge must be secure. If the window is creased the crease must be carefully examined for small perforations or splits.

4. The seam at the side of the facepiece must be secure and the stockinet strip firmly stuck down to the rubber.

5. The safety pins on the head harness must be present and in usable condition.

(b) *Container*

6. The container must show no signs of perforations, heavy denting or entry of water.

7. The inlet valve must not be perished or stiff and it must seat properly so that when the wearer breathes out it effectively prevents the breath from passing back into the container. If the valve is stiff or has lost its elasticity it must be replaced, but if it is curled up but still soft it can be removed from the stud, turned over and replaced.

(c) *Rubber Band and Assembly of Respirator*

8. The rubber band must not be perished, torn, nor showing surface cracking. Its condition can be judged by lifting it with the finger and thumb at one edge and testing its elasticity. While the rubber band is thus lifted it must be verified that the position of the container is correct according to the size of facepiece.

The correct positions are as follows:—

Large facepiece—edge of rubber just over the raised swage in the container body.

Medium and small facepieces—edge of rubber just up to the raised swage in the container body

The rubber band must be positioned so that its centre lies over the edge of the rubber of the face-piece. If the rubber band is in good condition it will return on to the container with a pronounced snap when it is released after the above inspection.

Note.—The container should not be removed from the facepiece unless there is definite reason to suspect a fault which cannot otherwise be investigated.

16. The Civilian Duty Respirator

The Civilian Duty respirator has been designed for members of civil air raid precautions services and others who might be called upon to carry out their normal duties in the presence of gas, but who are not likely to be continuously exposed to the highest concentrations.

The basic design (*see* Fig. 6) is the same as that of the Civilian respirator. The container is directly attached to the front of the facepiece.

There are three patterns of container in existence:—

(i) C.D. Mark I: a container made from a water-proofed cardboard cylinder on to which two light metal ends are seamed. Inside are activated charcoal and a particulate filter to prevent the passage of arsenical smokes. This pattern has a one-way valve at the outer end which is the inlet valve of the respirator. The inner end of the container is of perforated metal, and as this might be liable to become infected from the wearer's breath, and disinfection would be difficult without damaging the filters inside, an absorbent pad is

D

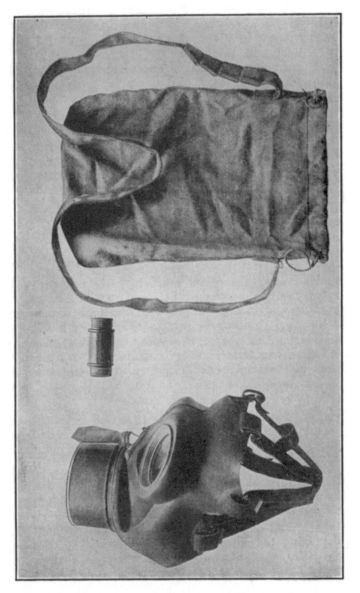

Fig. 6—Civilian Duty Respirator and Haversack.

provided and held with an annular spring clip, to protect the container from infection. When the respirator is disinfected this pad is thrown away, and a new one inserted.

(ii) C.D. Mark II: a container identical with Mark I except that the whole body of the container is of metal, lacquered black.

(iii) C.D. Mark III: an improved and slightly larger container, which is in fact identical with the container of the Civilian respirator except that the charcoal in it has a higher degree of activation. The main effect of this difference is that the container can absorb more gas before becoming saturated—i.e. that its effective life in use is longer. In this container the inlet valve is at the inner end, and can itself be disinfected, so that no absorbent pad is required as in the case of Mark I and II patterns. The Mark III container is distinguished from the Civilian respirator container by having a red band round the black lacquered body.

The facepiece is of stouter construction than in the case of the Civilian respirator (G.C. Mark II), to withstand harder wear. It is made of rubber, moulded to fit closely to the face. It is fitted with an outlet valve, and has a protuberance on the left cheek to which a microphone can be attached for those regularly employed on telephone work.

The facepiece is held in position on the face by elastic bands passing round the back of the head. These can be adjusted for fit and comfort by means of buckles.

The rubber of the facepiece fits tightly round the end of the container and is secured by means of a metal band, or, in earlier examples, by cord.

The eyepieces are made of strong plain glass discs fitted into metal rims, and are removable by unscrewing for decontamination purposes. To prevent dimming, the later patterns of facepiece have also a thin disc of gelatine-coated material inside the eyepiece. This is removable. When this gelatine disc is not fitted, particular attention must be paid to the application of anti-dimming compound.

An anti-dimming outfit is provided which consists of a cylindrical metal box containing anti-dimming compound and a piece of cloth. When properly applied this compound causes the moisture condensed on the eyepieces to form a clear film which does not interfere with the vision. The instructions for using this are printed on the box and are as follows:—

> " Clean eyepiece with cloth provided. Breathe on eyepiece and apply a little compound evenly with the finger. Breathe on eyepiece again and polish *very* lightly with the cloth so that a thin even film of the compound remains."

A small canvas haversack (*see* Fig. 6) is provided in which the complete respirator and anti-dimming outfit can be carried. This haversack has a webbing sling and is worn slung over the shoulder. In Figure 7 A and B a member of the St. John Ambulance Brigade is shown wearing the respirator slung and adjusted.

The drill for the Civilian Duty respirator is given in Appendix B.

17. The Service Respirator

The Service respirator is the pattern of respirator issued to the Fighting Services. The protection it affords is of the same kind as in the case of the Civilian and Civilian Duty respirators, but the duration of its efficiency against gas is longer, and it has been designed to allow the wearer the greatest possible freedom of movement and the maximum use of his faculties. For instance, the weight of the container is carried on the chest and not on the facepiece, and special attention has been paid to the prevention of dimming of the eyepieces.

A—Slung.   B—Adjusted.
Fig. 7—Civilian Duty Respirator.

The Service respirator will be provided for members of certain civil air raid precautions services whose duties might involve their remaining and working in high concentrations of gas (e.g., police, first aid parties, decontamination squads, etc.).

The container is a tinned iron box which contains activated charcoal for the absorption of gases, such as phosgene and mustard gas, and a particulate filter to prevent the passage of finely divided smokes like the arsenical gases.

The following types of container are being used, or will be used, with this respirator:—

Type A, in which the air enters the container through an inlet valve in the bottom of the

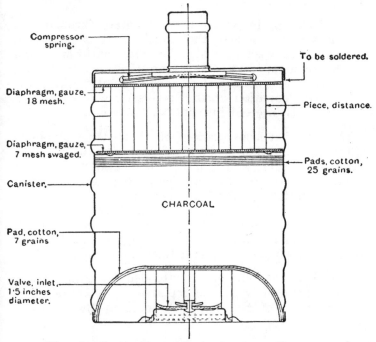

FIG. 8—SECTION OF CONTAINER OF SERVICE RESPIRATOR (TRAINING TYPE A).

canister. It is supported on a wire platform placed at the bottom of the container compartment of the haversack. The general construction of this container is illustrated diagrammatically in Figure 8.

Type D, in which the air enters through two inlet valves at the top of the canister. It is painted black with a distinguishing band of grey over the adhesive tape which seals the top of the canister to the body. The wire platform at the bottom of the haversack should be removed before inserting the container into its compartment. This process may be found a little difficult, because the fit is tight, but it can be accomplished with care.

Type E, in which the air enters through two slots in the side of the canister. It is painted a light yellowish brown. The wire platform should be removed from the haversack when using this container, and the slots should point towards the central partition of the haversack when the container is inserted into its compartment.

The internal construction of these three types is different, but the general principle on which they work is the same and is indicated diagrammatically in Figure 8. As regards efficiency they all give complete protection against non-persistent gases and the vapour of persistent gases, but the Type A container gives only a very limited protection against finely divided smokes, whereas the Type D and Type E afford adequate protection against these smokes.

The Type A container is intended for training purposes only, and would be replaced by a container of the standard of the Type D or E in the event of war.

If for any reason it becomes necessary to change the container, this can be done without difficulty.

The facepiece is made of rubber (sometimes covered on the outside with khaki stockinet) which is moulded to fit closely to the face. The gas-tightness of the respirator is dependent upon the closeness of this fit. It is held in position by elastic bands attached to the rubber which pass round the back of the head.

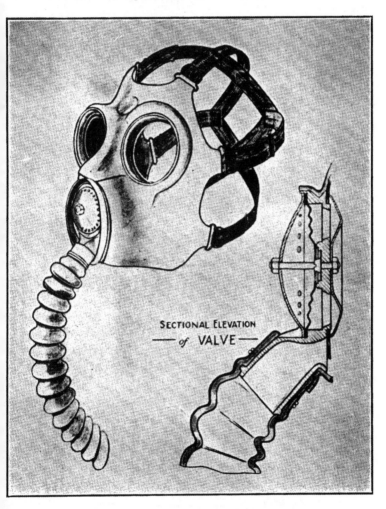

SECTIONAL ELEVATION
of VALVE

FIG. 9—FACEPIECE OF SERVICE RESPIRATOR.

These elastics are provided with buckles so that the lengths can be adjusted to suit each individual. As the facepiece is made in three sizes, no difficulty will normally be experienced in obtaining a satisfactory fit for an adult person.

The construction of the facepiece is illustrated in Figure 9.

.The eyepieces are made of splinterless glass. In the more recent patterns, the glasses can be removed by unscrewing to allow decontamination of the face-piece by boiling, which would damage the splinterless glass.

A valve holder (for the outlet valve) connects the facepiece to the flexible tube and contains the outlet valve. Air is drawn in from the container through the valve holder and along passages in the rubber wall of the facepiece to an inlet between the eyepieces. As a result of this arrangement, the air entering the facepiece passes across the eyepieces and so reduces the dimming caused by condensation from the expired air.

The air breathed out passes directly through the outlet valve to the outer atmosphere. This valve has been designed to render the speech of the wearer audible.

The flexible tube is made of rubber covered with stockinet; it is corrugated to give flexibility and to prevent its collapsing when bent. The ends are wired on to the valve holder at one end, and to the neck of the container at the other.

An anti-dimming outfit is provided as described for the Civilian Duty respirator (see Section 16).

The respirator is carried in a waterproof canvas haversack, the main part of which is divided into two compartments, one for the container and the other for the facepiece and anti-dimming outfit (*see* Fig. 10).

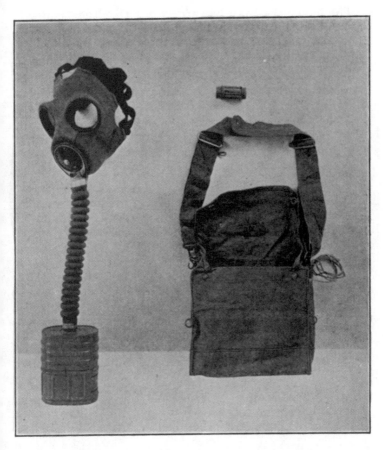

FIG. 10—SERVICE RESPIRATOR AND HAVERSACK.

The haversack may be carried in either the " slung " or " alert " position. When in the " slung " position the haversack is on the left side of the body with the sling over the right shoulder. This is illustrated in Figure 11 A. There are two methods of attaining the

A—SLUNG POSITION.   B—ALERT POSITION.
FIG. 11—SERVICE RESPIRATOR.

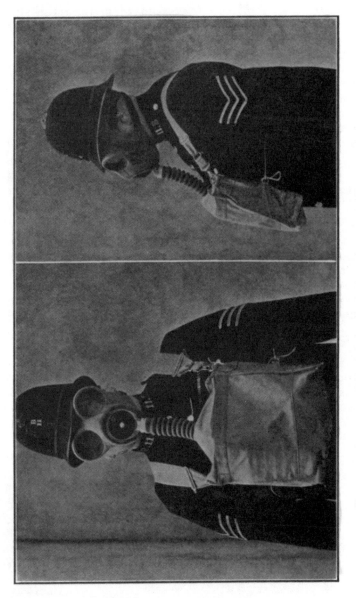

FIG. 12—SERVICE RESPIRATOR ADJUSTED, FRONT AND SIDE VIEWS.

" alert " position. In the standard method the sling is fastened behind the shoulders by means of the whipcord which is attached to one corner of the haversack. This method is described in detail in the drill which is given in Appendix C, and is illustrated in Figure 11 B. In the alternative " alert " position the sling is shortened by engaging the tab on the sling with the S hook at the side of the haversack. The haversack then remains on the chest supported from the neck and is secured to the body by means of the whipcord.

Figure 12 shows the respirator adjusted in the " gas " position, employing the standard " alert " position for the haversack.

18. The Care of Civilian Duty and Service Respirators

The general principles governing the care of Civilian Duty and Service respirators are the same as those already described for the Civilian respirator (Section 14). Owing to their different methods of construction the details to be attended to are different, and are described separately in this Section.

These respirators have been designed to withstand reasonable wear and tear during use, and if properly looked after, will last many years. Economy of respirators would be most important in war, and it is therefore essential that all to whom they may be issued should receive thorough training in the care, wearing, cleansing and methods of folding. The more serious causes of damage are—

(1) Water entering the container and affecting the efficiency of the charcoal and filter.

(2) Injury to the outlet valve which might allow gas to enter without passing through the container.

(3) Injury to the rubber facepiece or the elastic head harness.

(4) Prolonged storage in a folded condition without use.

Attention to the following points will result in a much longer life for the respirator:

(*a*) Respirators must be protected from wet, and when not in use should be kept if possible in a cool, dry, dark place.

(*b*) Prolonged storage of the respirator in the haversack tends to cause distortion of the facepiece and cracking of the rubber where it is folded. This can be prevented to a great extent by frequent wearing of the respirator. Where this is not feasible, as in storage, the facepieces should be taken out of the haversack at least once a month, and opened out to allow the rubber to recover its shape. (N.B.—This does not apply to facepieces packed separately from their containers, etc., for purposes of storage over a long period.)

(*c*) After use the harness and the inside of the facepiece should always be wiped dry before being put away. If wet from exposure to rain, the facepiece should not be put into the haversack until it is dry.

(*d*) In order to maintain the facepiece in a wholesome condition when in use, it should be periodically cleansed by sponging the whole of the inside with an approved disinfectant (see Appendix G), and subsequently wiping out with water. During this process care must be taken to prevent water entering the container. The respirator should then be allowed to dry before it is put away, and in the case of the Civilian Duty respirator with Mark I and II containers the gauze pad in front of the container should be renewed.

In addition the respirator should be disinfected twice a year, and on every occasion when the respirator changes ownership or if the owner contracts an infectious disease. The instructions for disinfection are contained in Appendices E and F.

(*e*) When a respirator is issued to an individual, great care should be taken that he is properly fitted by a competent person. The correct size of facepiece must be selected, and the headharness adjusted, to suit the requirements of the particular individual. Wherever possible the correctness of the fit should be tested by putting the person into a tear gas cloud with the respirator adjusted.

The processes for decontaminating Civilian Duty and Service respirators are described in Section 28.

19. Inspection of Civilian Duty and Service Respirators

Respirators in issue should be inspected frequently by a responsible person to ensure that they are in a satisfactory condition and are receiving the care and attention which they require. The inspector should pay special attention to the following points:—

CIVILIAN DUTY RESPIRATOR AND SERVICE RESPIRATOR.

(1) The elastic bands should be sound and sufficiently strong for their purposes, and buckles and loops should be firmly attached.

(2) The rubber facepiece must not be perished or torn. The presence of small holes may be detected by holding the facepiece up to the light and stretching the rubber gently.

(3) The eyepieces must not be damaged, and if of the screwed-in type they must be screwed tight. In all types the rims must be securely bound to the facepiece.

CIVILIAN DUTY RESPIRATOR.

(4) The outlet valve must be securely attached to the metal mounting, and must not be perished or punctured. By gently pulling the valve sideways and extending it about half an inch, any weakness will readily be seen.

(5) The container must be securely attached and must not be punctured or show signs of entry of water. The inlet valve must not be perished and must seat properly. If it is stiff it should be changed. If it is curled up but still soft it can be removed from the pin, turned over and replaced. The lever lid carrying the valve in Mark I and II types may be removed for inspection of the valve.

SERVICE RESPIRATOR.

(6) The valve holder must not be damaged and must be securely fixed in the facepiece.

(7) The valve guard must not be damaged.

(8) The corrugated tube must be sound and securely attached at both ends. If the container is attached at the wrong angle, the rubber tube may twist or become kinked, and the facepiece will not stay on the face properly. Hold the facepiece up by the valve holder, letting the container hang freely, in order to see that the container is in the correct position relative to the facepiece. When the facepiece is adjusted the container should hang with its widest side flat against the body.

(9) The container should show no signs of perforations, heavy denting or entry of water. The container neck should be securely attached to the body.

After the visual examination the valves should be tested in the following manner:—

Inlet valve.—Adjust the respirator to the face and close the outlet valve by pinching it or by covering the aperture, according to the type under test. Next attempt to breathe out. If air escapes, it is an indication that the inlet valve is defective, or that there is a leak in the connecting tube or container. Air may of course escape round the sides of the facepiece, but a defective inlet valve can easily be detected before the lifting of the facepiece occurs.

Outlet valve.—Adjust the facepiece as before. On pinching the connecting tube of the Service respirator it will not be possible to inhale if the valve is sound. In the Civilian Duty respirator, the normal entrance of air may be stopped by holding the palm of the hand firmly over the valve at the bottom of the Mark I and II container. In the case of Mark III type the perforated end may be closed by holding a piece of smooth cardboard or rubber firmly against it. If the outlet valve of the Civilian Duty respirator is stuck owing to saliva drying upon it, this can be remedied by rubbing the valve gently between the thumb and fingers.

Before replacing the Service respirator in the haversack, the latter should be examined to see that the sling, eyeletted canvas tab, S hook, press buttons, cord and D's are all sound. The presence of the anti-dim outfit should also be checked.

After Service respirators have been inspected, they should be adjusted to the face at the conclusion to make sure that the containers have been correctly replaced in the haversacks, so that the rubber tube is not kinked.

CHAPTER VI

PROTECTION OF THE BODY

20. Need for Protection of the Skin against Blister Gases

It has already been stated that the most dangerous gas likely to be met is mustard gas, or some other blister gas. For those who have to encounter such a gas for an appreciable time, the protection given by the respirator alone is not sufficient.

The respirator container will prevent blister gas vapour from passing through it. Thus a person wearing his respirator will have his face and respiratory system protected, but the remainder of his body will be liable to injury by the liquid or vapour. Ordinary clothing is of some value in that it delays penetration by vapour, and to a less extent liquid, and therefore the full effects of any contamination are not immediately produced on the skin. If such clothing is removed *quickly* and the skin thoroughly washed, damage may be entirely avoided, or at any rate very much reduced. The treatment is described in Chapter VII.

On the other hand, should it not be known that contamination has occurred, the clothing will be a source of grave danger, since it will maintain the gas in close proximity with the skin. By the time irritation is noticed, the blister gas will have penetrated well into the skin and the damage will have been done.

21. Anti-Gas Clothing

Whenever it is necessary for particular individuals to carry out essential work in places where they are likely to be exposed to either liquid mustard gas or high concentrations of the vapour, they must be protected by some form of clothing which the gas cannot penetrate. The best material for resisting the penetration of liquid mustard gas is oilskin of the type used in the Navy. This oilskin is manufactured from various textile materials by treating them with certain "drying" oils such as linseed oil.

It should be noted that the time taken by the liquid blister gas to get through this oilskin material in hot weather is about half the time taken in cold weather. This must be taken into account when deciding the safe limit of time for which articles of protective clothing may be worn. Naturally the time of penetration will vary for different grades of material, but the strong oiled wigan of which protective gloves are made will, when new, keep out liquid mustard gas for at least four hours even in hot weather. Garments of this material are decontaminated by boiling, which treatment reduces the penetration time. After being boiled, clothing should not be reckoned as capable of keeping out liquid blister gas for more than three hours.

The non-porous nature of this oilskin material causes the heat and perspiration from the body to be retained inside the clothing. In hot weather the amount of manual work that a person wearing oilskins can accomplish is consequently limited, owing to fatigue and exhaustion.

22. Patterns of Anti-Gas Garments

The various types of oilskin garments which have been adopted for A.R.P. services are as follows. The numbers in brackets are those of specifications prepared by the Technical Co-ordinating Committee on Textiles and Clothing, which (after the experimental stage) are published by H.M. Stationery Office.

(*a*) Jacket (Oilskin No. 1) anti-gas, heavy (T.C. 202).

(*b*) Trousers (Oilskin No. 1) anti-gas, heavy (T.C. 203).

(*c*) Hood, anti-gas (T.C. 226).

(*d*) Gloves, anti-gas (T.C. 225).

(*e*) Jacket, anti-gas, light (T.C. 229).

(*f*) Trousers, anti-gas, light (T.C. 229).

(*g*) Apron, anti-gas.

(*h*) Curtain, helmet, anti-gas.

In addition to the above oilskin garments the following anti-gas articles will be provided:

(*i*) Boots, rubber, knee. (T.C. 174.)

(*k*) Eyeshields. (L.A.G. 1174).

(A steel helmet to protect the head against splinters, etc., will be worn with the anti-gas garments by services with duties out of doors.)

Persons likely to be exposed to contact with liquid gas, but not to severe concentrations of vapour, e.g., undressers at First Aid Posts, will wear

(*d*) Gloves, anti-gas (unless a satisfactory lighter type can be evolved).

(*g*) Apron, anti-gas.

This garment is sleeved and protects the arms and front of body against liquid but not vapour. Under-clothing and a strong cotton suit or overall should be worn under it.

Persons not likely to be working for long in heavy concentrations of gas, but who nevertheless may require protection from both liquid and vapour will be provided with

The light anti-gas suit, which consists of

(*d*) Gloves, anti-gas.

(*e*) Jacket, anti-gas, light.

(*f*) Trousers, anti-gas, light.

(*h*) Curtain, helmet.

(*i*) Boots, rubber, knee

Underclothing and a strong cotton suit or overall should be worn under this suit.

There are certain categories of A.R.P. Services who may be required to carry out their duties in the worst concentrations of vapour in an area badly contaminated by liquid blister gas, e.g., decontamination squads. For these the maximum protection must be provided.

The full heavy anti-gas suit consists of the following:

(a) Jacket, anti-gas, heavy.

(b) Trousers, anti-gas, heavy.

(c) Hood, anti-gas.

(d) Gloves, anti-gas.

(i) Boots, rubber, knee.

Only underclothing should be worn under this suit.

A man equipped in the heavy anti-gas suit, but without the hood, is shown in Figure 13.

The hood, which is made of oiled fabric, is adjusted after the respirator is in position, to protect the exposed portions of the head and neck. Its use is only necessary when work has to be undertaken for prolonged periods in high concentrations of vapour, such as might be encountered in enclosed spaces, and it should seldom be necessary in the open air.

The eyeshield consists of a sheet of cellulose acetate which can be bent to suitable shape and fastened over the eyes by elastic bands passing round the back of the head. It is designed to protect the eyes against blister gas spray. Generally speaking it will be provided for services such as police and air raid wardens who may be expected to be in the streets at any time, but not for services such as decontamination and rescue workers who would remain indoors till summoned for duty and would then wear respirators.

The anti-gas helmet curtain is an oilskin veil, for attachment to the steel helmet, to protect the neck and ears against spray.

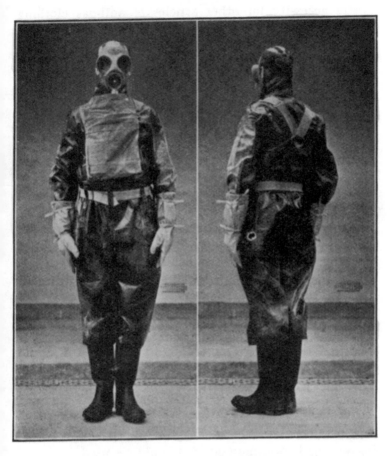

FIG. 13—MAN EQUIPPED WITH HEAVY ANTI-GAS
SUIT, WITHOUT HOOD.

23. Use of Anti-Gas Garments

Wherever there is any danger from vapour the
respirator must be worn, and if there is blister gas
on the ground, rubber boots are required. Leather
gives only a short period of protection, and is very
difficult to decontaminate.

The necessity for other articles of anti-gas clothing will depend on the particular circumstances and nature of the work to be undertaken.

Owing to the exhaustion caused by the heavy anti-gas suits they should not be worn unless the circumstances make it essential. Where adequate ventilation can be arranged to avoid dangerous concentrations of vapour, so that the only danger is from touching contaminated objects, the lesser forms of protection may be adequate and will cause much less reduction in efficiency. The apron should, for instance, be adequate for first aid personnel engaged merely in handling casualties who may be contaminated.

There are two methods of wearing the hood, jacket and trousers of the heavy suit, viz.: —

(a) Skirt of hood under the jacket, jacket inside the trousers and trousers inside the boots with a fold over the top of them; and

(b) Skirt of hood outside the collar of the jacket, jacket outside the trousers gathered in by a belt and secured in an air-tight fashion, and trousers outside the boots.

Protection against vapour is better in method (a) and this method should be used when there is no danger of liquid mustard gas entering the suit. When there is danger of liquid mustard gas running or being washed down the neck and/or inside the trousers or boots, method (b) should be used.

Protective gloves can be made of various qualities of oiled fabric according to the work for which they are intended. The gloves which are most suitable for general work have a separate thumb but all the fingers in one piece. These are cheap and easy to manufacture.

Before putting on the compete anti-gas suit, it will be necessary to remove the ordinary clothing and change into other underclothing. The wearing of anti-gas clothing will impose limits on the possible period of work. If work has to be carried on in a confined space with heavy vapour contamination present, necessitating the wearing of the complete outfit with hood, it is probable that only three spells of from half an hour to an hour could be performed during each 24 hours. This depends on the temperature. In cold weather, or in less severe concentrations which do not necessitate the wearing of the hood, men might be able to work for three spells of two hours.

The protection against blister gas vapour afforded by the heavy anti-gas suit is of limited duration, owing to the suction effect produced by movement. The inside of such suits should therefore be ventilated at regular intervals by opening the coat and letting down the trousers in an atmosphere free from blister gas vapour.

24. Order of Dressing and Undressing

The order of dressing in full anti-gas clothing should be as follows. Where possible another man should assist as a dresser.

(1) Attend to wants of nature.

(2) Remove own clothing, underclothing and socks.

(3) Put on clean underclothing and socks.

(4) Put on trousers.

(5) Put on boots.

(6) Put on jacket.

(7) Adjust respirator in Alert position.

(8) Put on gloves, which are tied at wrist by dresser.

(9) Put on helmet.

The hood should not be put on until after the respirator is adjusted in the Gas position, when gas is encountered.

After each period of work the anti-gas clothing should be removed by another man (himself suitably protected) and the wearer must wash thoroughly and change back into his own underclothing.

The various articles of clothing should be taken off in the following order:—

(1) Hood or helmet.
(2) Gloves.
(3) Respirator.
(4) Jacket or apron.
(5) Trousers lowered.
(6) Boots removed.
(7) Trousers removed.

These articles should each be placed in the appropriate covered bin as removed.

The man who is being undressed should then move his feet to the other side of the form on which he is sitting without letting them touch the floor, and take off his

(8) Underclothing

which he should put into an appropriate bin.

This move is necessary because the floor on which the boots and oilskin clothing are removed may have become contaminated as a result of successive persons undressing on it, and to stand on it with bare feet would be dangerous.

The bins for the contaminated clothing can be ordinary sanitary bins with lids, and different bins will be required for the following:—

(1) Boots.
(2) Anti-gas clothing.
(3) Respirators.
(4) Underclothing.
(5) Headgear, other than hoods.

CHAPTER VII

ANTI-GAS TREATMENT OF PERSONS

25. Anti-Gas Treatment of Persons

Mustard gas, or any other blister gas, has a serious effect on the skin of any person who comes in contact with it.

The contamination to which these gases give rise is really the same on persons as on things, and any process for removing it, whether by washing with water or the application of neutralising chemicals, may be rightly described as " decontamination " in either case. The premises and the personnel for dealing with persons must, however, in civil air raid precautions, be distinct from those connected with the removal of contamination from streets, buildings, and material objects generally, with the result that confusion is apt to arise if the word " decontamination " is used indiscriminately in relation to both aspects. It is therefore the practice to reserve the words " decontaminate " and " decontamination " for the removal of contamination from material objects, and to describe the removal of bodily contamination of persons as anti-gas treatment, or to use such neutral words as cleansing or washing. The facilities which must be specially provided for these purposes (except as regards the members of air raid precautions services, as described in the next Section) are to form part of the first aid organisation, and neither the places nor the personnel employed need be designated otherwise than as first aid posts and first aid personnel.

Any person who has become contaminated by blister gas through exposure to vapour or through contact with liquid, must be speedily treated to prevent his becoming a casualty. Even if the treatment is unavoidably delayed, it will in many cases reduce the severity of the injuries. But it cannot be over-emphasised that *speed of action is of the utmost importance.*

The first essential is to remove the clothing which has become contaminated and to dispose of it in such a way that it does not become a source of danger to others.

Contamination of the skin by liquid should be treated as follows:—

(i) When bleach ointment is *immediately* available it should be well rubbed into the contaminated area and then wiped off within two minutes.

(ii) If a paste of bleaching powder and water can be made available *within five minutes* the affected part of the body should be treated with this paste, which should be flushed off with water within two minutes.

In the case of either of the above treatments the contaminated persons should be thoroughly washed with hot water and soap as quickly as possible.

(iii) If neither bleach ointment nor bleach paste can be made available within five minutes of the contamination, *or while liquid contamination is still visible on the skin,* the individual should be undressed and washed with hot water and soap as soon as practicable, and redressed in clean clothing. *The bleach mixtures are only more efficacious than washing when they can be applied within five minutes of contamination.*

The bleach in either form will rapidly destroy mustard gas, but it will also irritate the skin if left in contact with it. Care must be taken to avoid bleach getting into the eye.

The washing can be done anywhere that hot water is available, and the sooner it is done the better. A First Aid Post is one possible place, and if it is known that serious liquid contamination has been sustained, it would in any case be best for the patient to go to a First Aid Post, after the first washing, for further advice and treatment.

In cases of vapour contamination of the skin the best treatment is washing with soap and hot water as soon as possible.

In all cases it will be an added safeguard to bathe the eyes with warm water.

The preceding paragraphs deal with cases in which definite contamination of the skin is known to have occurred. Whenever contamination is suspected, or is liable to have occurred, the general procedure should still be to undress and thoroughly wash the whole body with soap and warm water at the earliest opportunity. Fresh clothing should then be put on, and on no account must the contaminated clothing be worn again until it has been decontaminated as laid down in Section 27.

The mere process of washing and changing clothing can and should be undertaken by the public in their own homes or places of work if it can be managed sufficiently promptly. Recourse should only be had to a First Aid Post if no quicker means of washing are available, or if the contamination has been severe, and first aid treatment may be required.

The danger of causing further casualties by contaminated clothing which has been discarded requires stressing. Persons who intend treating themselves in their own homes must remove their boots and outer clothing before entering the house.

26. Preventive Cleansing for Members of Air Raid Precautions Services

As has already been made clear, the danger of mustard gas and similar blister gases is that either the liquid or the vapour can be absorbed by the skin without being detected at the time. The symptoms may not appear for several hours.

In the case of members of air raid precautions services who have been on duty in an area where mustard gas was present, it will be desirable for them to undergo cleansing treatment as soon as they come off duty, as a routine precaution, irrespective of whether any particular man believes himself to have been exposed to gas.

There should therefore be a cleansing place available for all members of air raid precautions services when they come off duty. Where convenient this should be at the station or depot on which they are based; but alternatively a central cleansing depot may be provided for groups of men stationed at neghbouring depots.

The requirements of a cleansing depot are explained in Appendix H. The routine should be that when the men come on duty they should take off their own clothing (including under-clothing) and put on other clothing provided for the purpose; and when coming off duty should discard their duty clothing (or, if it is contaminated, have it taken off by undressers), and wash themselves before putting on their own clothes once more. (This change of underclothing will be necessary whenever they have to wear oilskin anti-gas clothing, whether they encounter gas or not.)

Where a central cleansing depot is in use, the men should go to that place on first commencing their tour of duty, and put on their working clothes. Their own clothes would then be waiting for them when they finally returned to the cleansing station after work.

Undressers (themselves wearing some form of anti-gas clothing) should be available to take off the contaminated clothing of the men as they come off duty. Men who undress themselves may spread contamination from their clothes to their bodies.

The arrangements for dealing with the contaminated clothing should be as described in the following Chapter, unless it is decided that it is more convenient to decontaminate it on the spot.

CHAPTER VIII

DECONTAMINATION OF CLOTHING AND EQUIPMENT

27. Decontamination of Clothing

It is of the greatest importance that clothing which has been contaminated with a blister gas should be properly decontaminated before it is again worn. Where the contamination has been by vapour only, this is not difficult and the processes described below can be reliably carried out in the home or elsewhere. Where, however, the contamination has been by liquid, it is inadvisable for the decontamination to be undertaken elsewhere than in properly equipped premises, except perhaps in the case of the simpler articles. The handling of articles contaminated with liquid blister gas during the process of decontamination is itself a matter requiring care and precautions, and should only be undertaken by personnel equipped with suitable protective clothing.

Five methods of decontaminating clothing are available in principle. It is not necessary to describe here in detail the methods of using and controlling the special plant referred to.

(1) *Boiling in water*

In this process the blister gas is destroyed (decomposed) by the boiling water. The work must be carried out in a well-ventilated place to prevent the accumulation of a dangerous concentration of vapour. Sea water may be used.

(2) *By steam treatment in a high pressure steam disinfector*

This process operates partially by the evaporation of the blister gas by heat and vacuum treatment, followed by destruction of the remainder by means of pressure steam. It can be carried out only by the use of special plant, and in this case the vapour extracted must be led away to a place where it will do no harm.

The process involves the admission of steam at pressures up to 15 lbs. per square inch alternating with extraction of the vapour by vacuum. The total process for each batch of garments would last an hour.

Wet garments must first be dried before being subjected to this process, otherwise rotting may be caused. The drying process.may be carried out either by weathering (see below) or by hot air treatment in drying rooms. In the latter case the vapour escaping from the room is dangerous.

(3) *Baking in hot, dry air*

This process operates by the evaporation of the blister gas. Again a special plant is required, and the vapour extracted must be led to a place of safety.

Careful control of temperature is required during this process.

(4) *Washing with soap and water*

In this process the blister gas is removed mechanically from the article to the water. This method is only suitable for cases of vapour contamination.

(5) *Weathering*

This process consists simply of exposure to the open air for a suitable period, until the blister gas has evaporated, or until the article is dry enough to be be treated by steam (see above). If the article has been heavily contaminated, there may be some danger from vapour in its immediate proximity.

The choice of method to be adopted will depend upon the degree of contamination and the nature of the article contaminated.

Vapour Contamination only

The methods given under this heading should be used only where it is *known* that the garments have not been exposed to liquid contamination. If there is even a *possibility* of liquid contamination the methods of treatment given under the next heading should be adopted.

Outer garments of all sorts: boots and equipment.	Hang in the open air for at least 24 hours. If any garment or article still smells of gas after 24 hours, treat as for liquid contamination.
Light dresses and under-clothing.	Wash with soap and water for at least 15 minutes and rinse well.

Liquid Contamination

Woollen garments (including suitings and underwear), silk and wool mixtures and good quality artificial silk garments.	Boil in plain water for one hour, keeping the garments fully immersed. If the boiling process is carried out with laundry machinery the time of boiling can safely be reduced to less than one hour. If the garments are greasy, the time of boiling should be doubled. Alternatively use the high pressure steam treatment *if the garments are dry*.

Woollen garments, as well as silk and artificial silk, may be boiled provided that plain water alone is used, without the addition of any soap or alkalis, and that the garments are not stirred while boiling, though they may be gently prodded down, or turned over, with a stick.

Contrary to general belief, with these precautions woollen garments will not suffer serious shrinkage in the boiling process, unless they are of shoddy material in which the wool has not been shrunk, or has been stretched, before weaving. It is not improbable however that certain dyes may run, and the garment may have a blotched appearance afterwards.

All cotton and linen fabrics.	Boil for half an hour in water to which two ounces (one handful) of washing soda per gallon has been added. Keep the garments .fully immersed.
Heavier canvas fabrics.	Do. for one hour.

The presence of the soda will prevent deterioration of the fabric. It will however probably be impossible to prevent fading and running of the colours.

Oilskin, including anti-gas clothing.	Boil for half an hour in plain water. Keep the articles fully immersed.
Gumboots.	Do. for two hours.
Boots and other leather articles which would be injured by boiling water or steam.	Bake in hot dry air under carefully controlled conditions.

28. Decontamination of Respirators

The decontamination of respirators will depend on whether they have sustained vapour contamination only, or whether they have been splashed with liquid gas. In the latter event the respirator must be withdrawn at once, and replaced.

Vapour contamination

The occasions on which the general public would be likely to require to use their respirators (e.g., for

F

passing quickly through gas vapour in the street, or escaping from a damaged refuge) are most unlikely to result in the respirator becoming contaminated in any degree requiring decontamination. It will probably be impossible to detect any smell of vapour on the respirator. No treatment should therefore normally be necessary, though cases of prolonged vapour contamination may occur. As a precaution, however, Civilian respirators which have been used in blister gas should be hung, out of their cartons, for a period as opportunity offers. If they can be hung out of doors, but protected from rain, so much the better. Their owners must not, however, let themselves be parted from them.

Those provided with Civilian Duty or Service respirators, on the other hand, are likely *ipso facto* to have had to remain in gas in the course of their duty. If the gas was blister gas, both respirator and haversack should be hung separately in the open air, but protected from rain, until they are required for the next spell of work. Where possible, this airing should last for 24 hours. Meanwhile their owners can rely on their Civilian respirators in so far as there are no spare Civilian Duty or Service respirators available.

Respirators which still smell of blister gas after 24 hours' airing should be treated as for liquid contamination.

Liquid contamination

As the facepiece of the Civilian respirator, with its fixed transparent window, cannot be decontaminated by boiling, these respirators cannot be made serviceable after *liquid* contamination, and the facepieces must be destroyed. The containers should be detached and treated on the outside with a paste of bleaching powder and petroleum jelly, such as vaseline, for ten minutes, and then wiped clean.

The facepieces of Civilian Duty and Service respirators are fitted with removable eyepieces. If the respirator has sustained liquid contamination, the eyepieces and the container should be removed and treated with a paste of bleaching powder and petroleum jelly for ten minutes (this should be applied to the outside of the container only), and then wiped clean. The facepieces and other rubber parts (including the connecting tube of Service respirators) should be immersed in boiling water and kept boiling for three hours.

.·The haversack, if also wetted with liquid mustard gas, will require boiling for one hour in water to which soda has been added. Any leather tabs attached to it will have to be renewed subsequently, since the boiling treatment renders them hard and brittle.

29. Decontamination of Stretchers

The standard pattern of stretcher in use has wooden handles. In most cases the supporting material is canvas. Any leather fittings will add to the difficulties of decontamination and should be removed. The most important point is to avoid contamination as far as possible. To protect the stretcher from contamination it should be covered with a suitable oilskin sheet which can be readily decontaminated by boiling as laid down for protective clothing in Section 27.

Should the stretcher become contaminated in spite of this precaution, the canvas will have to be removed from the handles and immersed for one hour in boiling water to which soda has been added. The handles will require scrubbing with the paste made from bleaching powder and water, but they will not be safe for contact with the bare hands for some days. This delay can be avoided by fitting the handles with oilskin covers.

Stretchers which have only been contaminated by vapour should be allowed to air in the open when not in use, for 24 hours if possible.

APPENDIX A

THE FITTING AND USE OF THE CIVILIAN RESPIRATOR

A.—FITTING

The facepiece of the Civilian respirator readily adapts itself to the shape of the wearer's face and it is held in position by three easily adjustable straps. Fitting is therefore a simple matter of selecting the proper size of respirator and adjusting the straps to suit the wearer's head.

The respirator is made in three sizes, large, medium and small. The LARGE size is correct for most men's faces, and the MEDIUM size for most women's faces; the SMALL size is intended for children. The size is marked on one of the head straps.

The fitting can be carried out if necessary by the wearer himself, but it can be done more conveniently and quickly by a second person.

When fitting the respirator, a man should first try a Large size; a woman, youth or girl a Medium size; and a child a Small size. The respirator is to be put on as described below. Spectacles, if worn, must first be removed.

To put on the respirator

Hold the respirator by each of the side straps with the thumbs underneath the straps, so that the inside of the window is facing you. The respirator will thus hang from the straps in the proper position for putting on the face. Lift the respirator to the face, thrust the chin forwards into it and draw the straps over the top of the head as far as they will go. Let go of the straps and make any small adjustments which may be necessary, e.g., the edge of the rubber may be turned inwards under the chin, one of the straps may be twisted, or the facepiece may not be straight on the face.

Strap adjustment

When the respirator has been put on, make sure that the buckle is at the back of the head just below the crown so that the two side straps are roughly level. Then adjust the straps, keeping the buckle in the same correct position, so that the facepiece is in contact with the skin all round the face. In doing this, *particular attention should be paid to lifting the face-piece well up on the face so that it makes good contact under the chin.* The straps must not be made any tighter than is required to keep the respirator in place when the head is nodded or shaken.

Size

Next see that the size is right for the wearer. If the size is right and the straps are adjusted properly, the wearer's eyes will appear practically in the middle of the window and the eyebrows will be visible below the top of the window.

If the eyes are much above the middle of the window and the eyebrows cannot be seen, make certain that the respirator is properly lifted on to the face. If it is as high as it will comfortably go, a bigger size of the respirator is desirable. If a large size is already being worn it means that the wearer's face is of unusual length, but the respirator will still give complete protection.

If the eyes are much below the middle of the window and the facepiece clearly goes on to the face too far a smaller size is desirable.

It does not follow that a person will not be protected if a respirator is worn which is slightly too large or too small, but attention must be paid to providing the proper size for the wearer so as to make sure that there is as little discomfort as possible.

When the respirator is worn, the air breathed out passes out of the respirator between the edges of the rubber facepiece and the wearer's face. It is clear therefore that the more tightly the facepiece is fitted on to the face the more pressure will have to be exerted by the wearer in breathing out. This must be borne in mind when choosing the size for the wearer and in adjusting the straps. If the respirator is too small or if the straps are adjusted too tightly the effort of breathing out will be increased.

To test fitting.

If the respirator has been properly put on and properly fitted the only source from which air can be drawn by the wearer is through the container. This should be verified by stopping up temporarily the perforated end of the container in some convenient manner (e.g. by holding a piece of smooth cardboard or rubber firmly against it) while the wearer attempts to breathe in strongly. The facepiece should be sucked in against the face by this process and there should be no leakage around the edge of the facepiece.

When this test shows that fitting and putting on have been correctly done, draw a pencil line across each of the straps along the edge of the buckle to mark their adjustment.

The respirator is then to be removed in the following manner : —

To remove the respirator

Insert a thumb under the buckle at the back of the head and pull the buckle forwards over the top of the head so that the respirator is lowered downwards from the face (*see* Fig. 17).

The respirator must not be removed by grasping the container (or the edge of the rubber under the chin) and lifting it off upwards. The only method which is to be used is that described above.

Securing the adjustment

After fitting and removal of the respirator, the strap adjustment is to be made secure by pinning the ends of the straps to the portions between the buckle and the facepiece. The pencil marks must be in the same position after pinning as they were when the respirator was fitted.

B.—Use

Before any occasion arises to use the respirator, it should have been properly fitted, and the adjustment of the straps secured with safety pins, as described above.

The respirator must always be carried by its owner in time of war wherever he may be by day or night. He should pay constant attention to keeping it and carrying it so as to avoid damage (see Section 14).

Immediately gas is encountered, or the alarm " GAS " received, the respirator is to be put on as quickly as possible. This should be learned as a drill, as follows:—

(i) Hold the breath and throw off any head-gear (or hold it between the knees). Remove spectacles.

(ii) Pick up the respirator, and hold it in front of the face by each of the side straps with the thumbs underneath the straps (*see* Fig. 14).

(iii) Thrust the chin forwards into the respirator and draw the straps over the head as far as they will go (*see* Fig. 15).

(iv) Breathe out, and continue breathing in a normal manner.

(v) Adjust the respirator squarely and comfort-ably on the face (*see* Fig. 16), and run the fingers over the facepiece to make sure that edges are not doubled inwards or the straps twisted. The buckles should rest on the back of the head. Replace head-gear, and pick up the carton of the respirator.

FIG. 14—STARTING TO PUT ON THE CIVILIAN RESPIRATOR.

FIG. 15—THRUSTING THE CHIN INTO THE CIVILIAN RESPIRATOR.

Fig. 16—Adjusting the Civilian Respirator.

Fig. 17—Starting to remove the Civilian Respirator.

(vi) *When it is thought that gas may no longer be present,* the air must be tested for gas before the respirator is taken off. First take a fairly deep breath, then insert two fingers of one hand between the cheek and the facepiece, and lift it slightly away from the face. Sniff gently. If gas is detected or *if there is any doubt,* replace the facepiece at once and breathe out strongly to blow out any gas that might have leaked in during the test.

When taking off the respirator, be very careful to do it as described in A above, by drawing the headharness forward off the head. See Figure 17. *Never take it off the chin first.*

To Adjust a Civilian Respirator on another Person.

The following instructions are given for adjusting a respirator on another person who cannot do it for himself (a child, for instance, or someone who is injured). The procedure can be carried out on anyone who is sitting or lying, or on a small child who is standing—i.e. whose head is low enough to be below the shoulder-level of the person who is adjusting the respirator. It cannot normally be used on an adult who is standing erect.

The key to the fitting is the chin. Unless the chin is lodged in the chin hollow of the facepiece it is impossible to ensure that the facepiece is adjusted correctly.

(i) Fold back the headharness outside the facepiece. Grip the facepiece with both hands on either side of the chin-hollow, thumbs inward.

(ii) Stand behind the other person and draw the chin-hollow over his chin. As soon as it is in position slide the hands up the edge of the facepiece, catching the headharness on the way, and draw it over the head into position.

(iii) Adjust the tension of the headharness, and the edges of the facepiece.

APPENDIX B

16

THE FITTING AND USE OF THE CIVILIAN DUTY RESPIRATOR

A.—FITTING

The respirator is made in two sizes: the NORMAL size, which fits most men's and some women's faces; and the SMALL size which, in general, is most suitable for women and adolescents. The difference between the sizes lies only in the dimensions of the rubber facepieces. The size is marked on the outside of the facepieces on the right cheek.

The elastic headharness serves to hold the respirator against the face, and, to suit different heads, each elastic band can be adjusted in length by means of buckles.

The operation of fitting a respirator consists in—

(*a*) Selecting the correct size for the wearer's face, and

(*b*) Adjusting the elastic bands of the headharness, so that when it is worn, the respirator is gastight, comfortable, and stable on the face.

This cannot be done properly by the wearer himself; it should be carried out by a second person in the following manner:—

Operation 1.—Preliminary.

First slacken off all the elastic bands of the headharness, so that the ends are about one inch from the buckles, and then instruct the wearer to put on the respirator. If spectacles are worn they should first be removed. Then, while the respirator is in position on the face, tighten each of the elastic bands so that the facepiece is drawn into firm, but not uncomfortable, contact with the skin and, as near as can be judged, all the bands are exerting an equal pull. Make certain that the wearer's chin is fitting closely into the chin of the facepiece.

Operation 2.—Observe if the size is correct.

The size of the respirator is generally correct if the wearer's eyes appear roughly midway between the top and the bottom of the eyepieces. If the eyes are very much *below* the centre of the eyepieces in a NORMAL size, it must be exchanged for a SMALL size. Conversely, if the eyes are very much *above* the centre in a SMALL size, a NORMAL size is required. If the face is very abnormal, and the eye positions are not satisfactory in either size of respirator, the size adopted should be that which fits the more safely and comfortably when the head-harness has been properly adjusted as described below.

Operation 3.—Adjust the headharness.

The facepiece of the respirator is made of soft and flexible rubber so that it will naturally tend to shape itself to the face and make close contact with the skin without using strong pressure. It is not necessary, therefore, to wear the headharness very tight in order to obtain a gastight fit; in fact, if the elastic bands are drawn too tight they may actually cause leakage by stretching the rubber and so prevent it from taking the shape of the face. The headharness should be no tighter than is needed to hold the facepiece firmly on the face during the carrying out of all duties, without causing discomfort.

(i) Instruct the wearer to move the head fairly vigorously in all directions and note if the face-piece slips on the skin. If it does so, all the elastic bands should be gradually tightened until the respirator is firm.

(ii) Next instruct the wearer to bend the head slightly forward and nod several times. The face-piece should neither slip down on the face nor the point of the chin jump out of the chin pocket. If either of these movements occurs, the two top elastic bands which pass over the crown of the head should be tightened.

(iii) Now grasp the respirator with one hand round the string binding which secures the container into the facepiece, and attempt to pull it gently away from the face. If the facepiece is felt to leave the chin easily, the two bottom elastic bands which pass under the ears should be tightened until the wearer can feel no movement away from his chin when the container is thus pulled.

(iv) Ask the wearer to confirm that the respirator is comfortable and is not pressing unduly at any point.

Operation 4.—*Test for gastightness.*

Now that the respirator has been comfortably fitted it must be tested to make sure that no air can leak in between the facepiece and the face. Grasp the respirator with one hand round the string binding which secures the container into the facepiece and place the palm of the other hand firmly over the circular opening at the end of the container so that no air can enter, taking care not to move the respirator on the face. If the respirator is fitted with a Mark III container, the perforated end should be closed by holding a piece of smooth cardboard or rubber firmly against it. Instruct the wearer to attempt to breathe in and to say if the air is felt to leak in at any point around the facepiece. If any such leakage is reported it can often be confirmed by placing the ear close to the facepiece and listening for the hiss of the inrushing air. The exact position of the leak can be located by pressing the tips of the fingers lightly on the outside of the facepiece at the suspected point and noting when the leakage ceases. If leakage does occur at any point, the adjacent elastic band must be re-adjusted until the leakage ceases, remembering that the leakage *may* be due to excessive tightness of the elastic and that slight slackening off may allow the rubber to make better contact with the skin.

If the wearer normally uses spectacles, they may be worn under the respirator *provided that* it is ascertained with certainty that they do not cause leakage at the temples. Most spectacles now in use are not suitable for wearing with a respirator because of this leakage, but on the majority of faces the type having thin wire frames may safely be worn. Thick horn spectacles are not likely to be safe. When the respirator has been fitted as described above, instruct the wearer to put on the respirator over his spectacles. Then repeat the test for gastightness. If there is no leakage, or if there is only a minute leakage when the breath is drawn in so strongly *that the face-piece is sucked in against the face,* the wearer may use his spectacles with the respirator. A slight tightening or loosening of the elastic bands which are attached at the temples may be found to improve the fitting over spectacles, but no greater leakage than that described is permissible. The anti-dimming compound provided with the respirator must be used on *both* sides of the glass of the spectacles.

After the respirator has been worn for some time it may tend to fit farther on to the face due to the rubber facepiece becoming more pliable. If this occurs, and discomfort is caused thereby, the elastic bands of the headharness should be slightly loosened while the rubber is still warm on the face, and the test for gastightness repeated.

B.—Use

It is assumed that the respirator has already been fitted to the wearer—that is, that the headharness is correctly adjusted to fit his head.

1. *General.*—The respirator is carried in the haver-sack at the left side of the body, with the sling over the right shoulder, and so that the tucks in the sling are to the front.

When the haversack is new, the sling is of suitable length for persons of small stature. For persons of larger stature it should be increased in length, by releasing one or more of the four tucks, so that the respirator hangs over the bone of the left hip. The tucks are released by carefully cutting the stitches.

2. *When it is known that there is no gas in the vicinity, or when there is no likelihood of gas being encountered,* the respirator is carried in the *NORMAL* position which is as follows (*see* Fig. 18 A):—

Respirator in haversack.

Haversack tightly closed and whipcord loops tied together in a double bow.

Haversack at left side and as far round the back of the wearer's body as is convenient and comfortable.

3. *When the presence of gas in the vicinity is suspected, or when there is a likelihood of gas being encountered* (e.g., during an air raid) the respirator is to be carried in the *ALERT* position, which is as follows (*see* Fig. 18 B):—

Respirator in haversack.

Mouth of haversack opened to its fullest extent.

Haversack on left hip, and clear of all other equipment so that it can be readily swung to the front of the body.

4. *Immediately gas is encountered, or the alarm " GAS " received,* the respirator is to be put on as quickly as possible. Rapid protection can be obtained only by following the correct details of respirator drill, which are as follows:—

(i) Hold the breath.

(ii) With the left hand grasp the bottom of the haversack and swing it to the front of the body. With the right hand remove any headgear and place it between the knees (*see* Fig. 19).

A—NORMAL POSITION. B—ALERT POSITION.
FIG. 18—C.D. RESPIRATOR BEING CARRIED

FIG. 19—CIVILIAN DUTY RESPIRATOR—ACTION ON
ALARM "GAS", STAGE ONE.

G

FIG. 20—CIVILIAN DUTY RESPIRATOR—ACTION ON
ALARM "GAS", STAGE TWO.

(iii) Thrust the right hand into the mouth of the haversack, and take hold of the respirator round the outside of the string binding, which secures the container to the facepiece.

Withdraw the respirator with a smart movement and hold it up in front of the face ready for putting on (*see* Fig. 20).

(iv) Insert the left thumb under the centre of the headharness at the point where the two lower elastic bands are attached, and allow the respirator to hang. Insert the right thumb beside the left and then slide the thumbs wide apart along the two adjacent elastic bands on each side (*see* Fig. 21).

(v) Bring the respirator towards the face. Dig the chin into it, and draw the respirator on to the face by passing the headharness smartly over the head with the thumbs.

(vi) Breathe out and continue breathing in a normal manner.

(vii) Adjust the respirator squarely and comfortably on the face and run the fingers over the facepiece to make sure that the edges are not doubled inwards, or the elastic bands twisted. The centre of the headharness should rest on the back of the head.

(viii) Replace headgear (*see* Fig. 22).

In the case of men wearing caps, helmets, or sou' westers with the chinstraps down, the head-dress should be removed and hung on the left forearm until the adjustment of the respirator is complete, when it should be replaced with the chinstrap at the back of the head.

FIG. 21—CIVILIAN DUTY RESPIRATOR—ACTION ON
ALARM "GAS", STAGE THREE.

FIG. 22—CIVILIAN DUTY RESPIRATOR FULLY
ADJUSTED AFTER ALARM "GAS".

IMPORTANT.

When removing the respirator from its haversack, it should never be withdrawn by pulling on the container alone. This might lead to breakage of the joint between the facepiece and container.

5. *When it is thought that gas may no longer be present,* the air must be tested for gas before the respirator is taken off. First take a fairly deep breath, then insert two fingers of the right hand between the cheek and the facepiece, and lift it slightly away from the face. Sniff gently. If gas is detected, or *if there is any doubt,* replace the facepiece at once and breathe out strongly to blow out any gas which might have leaked in during the test.

6. *When the air is known to be clear of gas,* the respirator may be removed. Raise the headgear with the left hand, insert two fingers of the right hand under the chin of the facepiece and lift the respirator off with an upward and backward movement over the head. Replace headgear (with the chinstrap under the chin in the case of men wearing caps, helmets or sou'westers with the chinstrap down).

7. *After using the respirator,* the inside of the facepiece should be wiped dry with a clean cloth before it is put away. If possible, the eyepieces should also be treated with anti-dimming compound so that the respirator is ready for the next emergency, but if conditions do not permit of an immediate treatment *the first available opportunity of doing so must be taken.*

To Replace the Respirator in the Haversack.

Hold the respirator in the right hand, thumb on one eyepiece, fingers on the other, with the container in the palm of the hand.

Fold in the forehead portion so that it separates the eyepieces.

Squeeze the eyepieces together and replace the respirator in the haversack, forehead portion first, harness buckles to the wearer's right.

To Adjust a Civilian Duty Respirator on another Person.

The following instructions are given for adjusting a Civilian Duty respirator on another person who cannot do it for himself (if, for instance, he is injured) The procedure can be carried out on anyone who is sitting or lying. It cannot normally be used on anyone who is standing erect.

The key to the fitting is the chin. Unless the chin is lodged in the chin-hollow of the facepiece it is impossible to ensure that the facepiece is adjusted correctly.

(i) Slip both hands into the facepiece from above, palms facing, finger tips almost in the hollow for the chin, thumbs extended and supporting the harness. The edges of the facepiece can be conveniently steadied between the forefinger and middle finger. The backs of the hands and fingers are thus against the rubber of the facepiece and the side straps of the harness.

(ii) Get the man's chin into the chin hollow, and as soon as it is in position slip the hands out, up either side of his face, catching the harness on the way, and slipping it over the head.

(iii) Adjust the harness tension and the edges of the facepiece.

17

APPENDIX C

THE FITTING AND USE OF THE SERVICE RESPIRATOR

A.—FITTING

The facepiece of the Service respirator is made in three sizes: the NORMAL size which fits most men's faces and some women's faces; the LARGE size which may be required for some men; and the SMALL size which in general is most suitable for women and adolescents. The difference between the sizes lies only in the dimensions of the rubber face-piece. The size is marked on the inside of the face-piece over the nose, and also outside on the stockinet under the chin.

The elastic headharness serves to hold the respirator against the face, and, to suit different heads, each elastic band can be adjusted in length by means of buckles.

The operation of fitting a respirator consists in—

(a) selecting the correct size for the wearer's face,

(b) adjusting the elastic bands of the head-harness, so that when it is worn, the respirator is gastight, comfortable, and stable on the face.

This cannot conveniently be done by the wearer himself; it should be carried out by a second person in the following manner:—

Operation 1.—Preliminary

First slacken off all the elastic bands of the head-harness, so that the ends are about one inch from the buckles, and then instruct the wearer to put on the respirator. If spectacles are worn they should first be removed. Then, while the respirator is in position on the face, tighten each of the elastic bands so that the facepiece is drawn into firm, but not uncomfortable, contact with the skin and, as near as can be judged, all the bands are exerting an equal pull. Make certain that the wearer's chin is fitting closely into the chin of the facepiece.

Operation 2.—Observe if the size is correct

The size of the respirator is generally correct if the wearer's eyes appear roughly midway between the top and the bottom of the eyepieces. If the eyes are much *below* the centre of the eyepieces in a NORMAL size it must be exchanged for a SMALL size. If the eyes are much *above* the centre in a NORMAL size then a LARGE size is required.

Operation 3.—Adjust the headharness

The facepiece of the respirator is made of soft and flexible rubber so that it will naturally tend to shape itself to the face and make close contact with the skin without using strong pressure. It is not necessary therefore, to wear the headharness very tight in order to obtain a gastight fit; in fact, if the elastic bands are drawn too tight they may actually cause leakage by stretching the rubber and so prevent it from taking the shape of the face. The headharness should be no tighter than is needed to hold the facepiece firmly on the face during the carrying out of all duties, without causing discomfort.

(i) Instruct the wearer to move the head fairly vigorously in all directions and note if the facepiece slips on the skin. If it does so, all the elastic bands should be gradually tightened until the respirator is firm.

(ii) Next instruct the wearer to bend the head slightly forward and nod several times. The facepiece should neither slip down on the face nor the point of the chin jump out of the chin pocket. If either of these movements occurs, the two top elastic bands which pass over the crown of the head should be tightened.

(iii) Now grasp the facepiece with one hand round the valve holder and attempt to pull it gently away from the face. If the facepiece is felt to leave the chin easily, the two bottom elastic bands which pass under the ears should be tightened until the wearer can feel no movement away from his chin when the facepiece is thus pulled.

(iv) Ask the wearer to confirm that the respirator is comfortable and is not pressing unduly at any point.

Operation 4.—*Test for gastightness*

Now that the respirator has been comfortably fitted it must be tested to make sure that no air can leak in between the facepiece and the face. Grip the connecting tube near its lower end and squeeze it tightly so that no air can be drawn through it. Instruct the wearer to attempt to breathe in and to say if air is felt to leak in at any point around the facepiece. If any such leakage is reported it can often be confirmed by placing the ear close to the facepiece and listening for the hiss of the inrushing air. The exact position of the leak can be located by pressing the tips of the fingers lightly on the outside of the facepiece at the suspected point and noting when the leakage ceases. If leakage does occur at any point, the adjacent elastic band or bands must be readjusted until the leakage ceases, remembering that the leakage *may* be due to excessive tightness of the elastic and that a slight slackening off may allow the rubber to make better contact with the skin.

If the wearer normally uses spectacles, they may be worn under the respirator *provided that* it is ascertained with certainty that they do not cause leakage at the temples. Most spectacles now in use are not suitable for wearing with a respirator because of this leakage, but on the majority of faces the type having thin wire frames may safely be worn. Thick horn spectacles are not likely to be safe. When the respirator has been fitted as described above, instruct the wearer to put on the respirator over his spectacles. Then repeat the test for gastightness. If there is no leakage, or if there is only a minute leakage when the breath is drawn in so strongly *that the facepiece is sucked in against the face,* the wearer may use his spectacles with the respirator. A slight tightening or loosening of the elastic bands which are attached at the temples may be found to improve the fitting over spectacles, but no greater leakage than that described is permissible. The anti-dimming compound provided with the respirator must be used on *both* sides of the glass of the spectacles.

B.—Use.

It is assumed that the respirator has already been fitted to the wearer—that is, that the headharness is correctly adjusted to fit his head.

1. *General.*—The respirator is carried in the haversack, the container being in the smaller (right hand) compartment and the facepiece in the larger compartment together with the anti-dimming outfit. The container must be inserted so that when the facepiece is worn the connecting tube is not twisted or kinked.

·2. *When it is known that there is no gas in the vicinity, or when there is no likelihood of gas being encountered,* the respirator is carried in the SLUNG position as follows:—

Respirator in haversack.

Haversack press buttons closed.

Haversack at left side of the body (press buttons next to body) and sling over the right shoulder, the length of sling being adjusted by the brass slide to suit the wearer's comfort. Haversack to be on top of any other equipment being worn.

3. *When the presence of gas in the vicinity is suspected, or when there is likelihood of gas being encountered* (e.g., during an air raid) the respirator is to be brought to the ALERT position as follows:—

(i) Swing haversack to front of body and bring left arm through sling so that haversack hangs straight down from the neck.

(ii) Undo press buttons with sharp pull.

(iii) Raise haversack on to chest, allowing sling to fall down the back.

(iv) Withdraw whipcord from haversack, pass through " D " ring on right side of haversack, through the sling behind the back and fasten to " D " ring on left side of haversack with a slip knot.

(v) Fold haversack flap over between haversack and body.

4. *Immediately gas is encountered, or the alarm " GAS " is received,* the facepiece is to be put on as quickly as possible. Rapid protection can be obtained only by following the correct details of respirator drill, which are as follows:—

(i) Hold the breath.

(ii) Remove headgear and place between the knees.

(iii) Lift the flap of the haversack. With the right hand seize the facepiece by the valveholder, pull it out of the haversack and turn it towards the face ready for putting on.

(iv) Insert the left thumb under the centre of the headpad by passing it under the point where the two bottom elastic bands are attached, and allow the facepiece to hang by the headharness. Insert the right thumb beside the left thumb and then slide the thumbs wide apart along the two adjacent elastic bands on each side.

(v) Bring the facepiece towards the face. Dig the chin into it, and draw it on to the face by passing the harness smartly over the head with the thumbs.

(vi) Breathe out and continue to breathe in a normal manner.

(vii) Adjust the facepiece squarely and comfortably on the face and run the fingers over it to make sure that the edges are not doubled inwards nor the elastic bands twisted.

The pad of the harness should be centrally positioned at the back of the head.

(viii) Replace headgear.

In the case of men wearing caps, helmets, or sou' westers with chinstraps down, the head-dress should be removed and hung on the left forearm until the adjustment of the facepiece is complete, when it should be replaced, with the chinstrap at the back of the head.

5. If gas is encountered or the alarm " GAS " is received *when the respirator is being carried in the " SLUNG " position,* protection can be obtained as follows : —

(i) Hold the breath. Remove headgear and place between the knees.

(ii) Swing the haversack to the front of the body and slip the left arm through the sling Undo the press buttons with a sharp pull.

(iii) Bend forward and withdraw the facepiece and adjust it as detailed above in 4 (iii) to (viii).

(iv) When protection has been obtained bring the haversack to the ALERT postion in the usual way.

In the case of men wearing caps, helmets or sou' westers with chinstraps down, the head-dress should be removed and hung on the left forearm after the left arm has been slipped through the sling, and replaced with the chinstrap at the back of the head when the adjustment of the facepiece is complete.

6. *When it is thought that gas may no longer be present,* the air must be tested for gas before the facepiece is taken off. First take a fairly deep breath, then insert two fingers of the right. hand between the cheek and the facepiece and lift it slightly away from the face. Sniff gently. If gas is detected, or *if there is any doubt,* replace the facepiece at once and breathe out strongly to blow out any gas which might have leaked in during the test.

7. *When the air is known to be clear of gas,* the facepiece may be removed. Raise the headgear with the left hand, insert two fingers of the right hand under the chin of the facepiece and lift it off with an upward and backward movement over the head. Replace headgear (with the chinstrap under the chin in the case of men wearing caps, helmets or sou'-westers with the chinstrap down).

8. *After using the respirator,* the inside of the face-piece should be wiped dry with a clean cloth before it is put away. If possible, the eyepieces should also be treated with anti-dimming compound so that the respirator is ready for the next emergency, but if conditions do not permit of an immediate treatment *the first available opportunity of doing so must be taken.*

To Replace the Facepiece in the Haversack.

Hold the facepiece in the right hand, thumb on one eyepiece, fingers on the other, with the valve-holder in the palm of the hand.

Fold in the forehead portion so that it separates the eyepieces.

Squeeze the eyepieces together and replace the facepiece in the haversack, forehead portion first, harness buckles to the wearer's right. Fold over the haversack flap between the haversack and the body.

To Adjust a Service Respirator on another Person.

The instructions given at the end of Appendix B for adjusting a Civilian Duty respirator on another person will apply also to the Service respirator, except that the placing of the haversack presents a further difficulty. This may be met by the following procedure:—

Bring his haversack to the front of his chest, with the sling in the usual Alert position, but do not waste time, at this stage, in tying the whip-cord. Take the facepiece out of the haversack, and hold it with the outlet valve towards you.

After this, the procedure will be as described in Appendix B, the last step being to make secure the adjustment of the sling of the haversack.

APPENDIX D

DISINFECTION OF CIVILIAN RESPIRATORS

Whenever it changes ownership, or in the event of an outbreak of infections disease, the respirator will be disinfected in the following manner:—

(1) Remove the rubber band, disconnect the container from the facepiece and remove the rubber disc valve from the container.

(2) Immerse the entire facepiece, the valve and the rubber band in a 2 per cent. solution of Formalin* for 30 minutes. Then remove them from the disinfecting solution and wash under running water for 5 minutes, or in several changes of water if running water is not available. Then hang up the facepiece, valve and band to dry.

(3) Hold the container by the rim on the outer end and sponge over the inner end and rim and the entire surface of the cylindrical body with cotton wool or a soft cloth which has been immersed in a 2 per cent. solution of Formalin and freed from excessive liquid. Allow to stand for 5 minutes and then wipe off the disinfecting solution with a soft cloth or sponge which has been wrung out in clean water. Then allow the container to dry. Care must be taken not to allow any liquid to enter the container during these operations.

(4) When all the parts of the respirator are dry they are ready for reassembly.

The respirator is to be reassembled in the following manner:—

(i) Replace the rubber disc valve on the stud in the container end.

---

* NOTE.—The disinfectants approved for use with the Civilian Duty and Service respirators may not be used with the Civilian respirator.

(ii) Grasp the container by the rim on its outer end and insert one side of the inner end into the aperture in the facepiece at a point immediately under the window. If the facepiece is a Large size, the edge of the rubber should be brought just over the raised swage in the container body, and if it is either a Medium or Small size the edge of the rubber should be brought just up to the raised swage. Hold the rubber in place on the container with the fingers, insert the fingers of the other hand inside the facepiece and stretch the rubber outwards and slip it over the container.

If the facepiece has not been slipped over the container far enough it must *not* be corrected by pulling the edge of the rubber; the fingers are to be inserted in the facepiece and the rubber lifted and *pushed* on to the container. See that the edge of the rubber is not turned in, that it is straight round the container, and in the correct position according to the size of the facepiece.

(iii) Place the rubber band in position around the container so that one half of its width lies on the rubber of the facepiece and the other half on the container.

H

APPENDIX E

DISINFECTION OF CIVILIAN DUTY RESPIRATORS

The stores required for disinfection of each respirator are:—

An approved disinfectant (see Appendix G).

Cloths, disinfecting, facepiece—2.

Pads, disinfecting—1 (for Mark I or II containers only).

A.—Normal Procedure

A solution of approved disinfectant will be prepared in the dilution specified in Appendix G. The solution should be freshly prepared for use on each occasion, and not more than 100 facepieces should be disinfected with three gallons of the solution.

Turn the facepiece completely inside out and sponge out the entire inner surface of the facepiece, including the eyepieces, and the top of Mark III containers (but not Mark I or II), with the disinfecting solution.

Turn the facepiece back to its normal shape and pour a little of the solution into the depression between the eyepieces. Then, pinching the outlet valve between the fingers, carefully tilt the mask so that the disinfecting liquid flows into the valve. When the valve is filled, release it and allow the liquid to drain away through the valve. Any solution remaining in the mask should be emptied out, care being taken not to wet the gauze pad on the Mark I or II container more than necessary.

Set the mask aside and proceed as above with other masks, arranging the routine so that each facepiece stands with a film of the disinfecting solution on it for at least five minutes.

After the facepiece has stood for five minutes, repeat the procedure above with clean water instead of the solution and sponge out the whole of the inside surface of the facepiece and the top of the Mark III container (but not Mark I or II) with water.

Wipe the inside of the facepiece with a clean cloth, disinfecting, and set it aside to dry off thoroughly at room temperature. Remove and throw away the disinfecting pad of the Mark I or II containers.

In the case of Mark I and II containers, before putting them away, the perforated top is to be wiped over with a cloth wrung out in the solution, allowed to stand for at least five minutes and then wiped over with a cloth wrung out in water. Care must be taken not to allow liquid to run into the perforations. Finally, a new pad, disinfecting, is to be fitted and secured in place with the spring.

B.—PROCEDURE IN THE EVENT OF AN EPIDEMIC OR OCCURRENCE OF INFECTIOUS DISEASE

In the event of an epidemic, the procedure described in A, above, will be immediately discontinued, and respirators will be disinfected according to the following procedure:—

A solution of approved disinfectant will be prepared, in the dilution specified in Appendix G. The solution should be freshly made for use on each occasion, and not more than 50 facepieces should be disinfected with three gallons of the solution.

The container will be detached by removing the turns of binding wire or cord. The wire or cord is to be destroyed. The container will then be removed by gently withdrawing it from the aperture of the facepiece with a slight turning movement.

In the case of Mark I and II containers, the pad, disinfecting, will be removed and destroyed.

The eyepieces and eyepiece rims are to be removed.

The whole of the facepiece, the eyepieces, the eyepiece rims and (in the case of Mark I and II containers) the spring retaining the pad, disinfecting, are then to be completely immersed in the disinfecting solution. Any convenient vessel may be used to accommodate a number of facepieces at one time.

After five minutes the facepiece, eyepieces, eyepiece rims and spring are to be removed from the disinfecting solution and thoroughly washed with water.

As much water as possible will be shaken off the facepiece. The whole facepiece, and the eyepieces, eyepiece rims and spring will then be laid out to dry. The facepiece must be quite dry before re-attaching the container.

The container is to be wiped over with a cloth wrung out in disinfecting solution, allowed to stand for five minutes, and then wiped over with a cloth wrung out in water. Care must be taken not to allow liquid to run into the perforations.

After disinfection, and when dry, the eyepieces will be re-assembled and the container must be re-attached as follows :—

The top end of the container is to be inserted in the central aperture of the facepiece and gently pressed inwards with a slight turning movement until the metal rim of the container is in contact with the flange at the base of the cylindrical aperture in the facepiece. The container is secured by binding with wire on to the outside of the rubber below the flange.

In the case of Mark I and II containers, a new pad, disinfecting, is then to be fitted and secured in place with the spring.

APPENDIX F

DISINFECTION OF SERVICE RESPIRATORS

All these respirators will be disinfected twice yearly and on every occasion that the facepiece changes ownership.

The stores required for disinfection of each respirator are:—

An approved disinfectant (see Appendix G).

Cloths, disinfecting, facepiece—2.

A.—NORMAL PROCEDURE

The procedure for disinfection, which will be carried out in two operations, is as follows:—

A solution of the approved disinfectant, in the dilution specified in Appendix G, will be prepared. The solution should be freshly prepared for use on each occasion, and not more than 100 facepieces should be disinfected with three gallons of the solution.

Sponge out the entire inner surface of the facepiece (including the eyepieces) with the disinfecting solution, taking care not to allow the liquid to enter the air inlet orifices which are at the sides of the eyepieces in Facepiece Mk. III and between the eyepieces in Facepiece Mk. IV.

Turn the facepiece completely inside out, so that a cup-shaped depression is formed over the outlet valve.

(a) For Facepiece Mk. III.—Nip the outlet valve between the fingers and pour into the cup-shaped depression about two fluid ounces of the disinfecting solution.

Swill the solution round gently, then release the outlet valve and allow as much of the solution as possible to drain out through the valve. Any solution remaining in the mask should be emptied out.

(*b*) For Facepiece Mk. IV.—Close the air inlet orifice between the eyepieces by inserting the thumb carefully in the hole. Pour about two fluid ounces of the disinfecting solution into the cup-shaped depression over the expiratory valve and swill round. If the solution does not pass out through the valve, tilt the facepiece over and allow the liquid to escape.

Set the facepiece aside and proceed as above with other facepieces, arranging the routine so that each facepiece stands with a film of the disinfecting solution on it for at least five minutes.

After the facepiece has stood for five minutes, repeat the procedure at (*a*) or (*b*) with clean water instead of the solution, and sponge out the whole of the inside surface of the facepiece with water.

Wipe the inside of the facepiece with a clean cloth, disinfecting, and set it aside to dry off thoroughly at room temperature.

Care must be taken as far as possible to avoid wetting the stockinet covering of the mask, as this requires a long time to dry.

In no circumstances must water or disinfecting solution be allowed to enter the air inlet orifice in the facepiece.

B.—PROCEDURE IN THE EVENT OF AN EPIDEMIC OR OCCURRENCE OF INFECTIOUS DISEASE

In the event of an epidemic, the procedure described in A, above, will be immediately discontinued, and facepieces will be disinfected by the following procedure.

A solution of the approved disinfectant, in the dilution specified in Appendix G, will be prepared. The solution should be freshly made for use on each occasion, and not more than 50 facepieces should be disinfected with three gallons of the solution.

The rubber connecting tube will be detached from the container, and the whole facepiece, with connecting tube, immersed in the disinfecting solution. Any convenient vessel may be used to accommodate a number of facepieces at one time.

After five minutes the facepiece is to be removed from the disinfecting solution and thoroughly washed out with water.

As much water as possible will be shaken off the facepiece and out of the connecting tube. The whole facepiece will then be laid out to dry. The time taken to dry will vary with the time of year, but it is essential that all moisture is allowed to dry out of the connecting tube before replacing on the container.

In addition, the inside of the neck of the container will be carefully wiped out with a rag moistened with the solution, the greatest care being taken to prevent any of the solution from penetrating to the chemicals in the container.

After disinfection, the rubber connecting tube should be re-attached to the container with wire binding.

§ 18]

APPENDIX G

DISINFECTANTS FOR CIVILIAN DUTY AND SERVICE RESPIRATORS

The following is a list of disinfectants which have been tested and approved for use in the cleansing and disinfection of Civilian Duty and Service respirators:—

	Concentration to be used for	
Disinfectant.	(a) *Cleansing.*	(b) *Disinfection.*
Goodhalls P.H. ...	$\frac{1}{3}$% solution	2% solution.
Monsanto White Disinfectant Fluid No. 1.	do.	do.
Izal	$\frac{1}{2}$% solution	3% solution.
Jeyes' White Cyllin	do.	do.
Kilcrobe W.O. Disinfectant Fluid.	do.	do.
Kolium W.O. Disinfectant Fluid.	do.	do.
Lawes' L.W. 4 White Oil Fluid.	do.	do.
McDougall's Municipal Disinfectant Fluid.	do.	do.
W.O. Disinfectant Fluid " Arnfield."	do.	do.
White Bactocene Disinfectant Fluid.	do.	do.
White Killgerm ...	do.	do.
White Septol Disinfectant Fluid.	do.	do.
Acrosone	$\frac{2}{3}$% solution	4% solution.

As a ready means of measuring small percentages, $1\frac{1}{2}$ eggcupsful to 3 gallons may be taken as equivalent to $\frac{1}{3}$ per cent. and 2 eggcupsful as $\frac{1}{2}$ per cent.

NOTE.—None of these disinfectants may be used with the Civilian respirator.

APPENDIX H [§ 26

Cleansing Depot for Air Raid Precautions Services

The accommodation described in this Appendix is intended to be applicable to all services which would be liable to be exposed to serious concentrations of gas—police, fire brigades, first aid parties, rescue parties, decontamination squads, and so on.

It is assumed that these facilities will be incorporated or improvised in existing buildings—police and fire stations, highway depots, etc. Space for the purpose should be provided in new buildings when they are erected. It can be used for other purposes, e.g., as store rooms, in time of peace.

The facilities required consist essentially of an open shed or other space for the removal of outer clothing, and then three rooms (undressing, washing and dressing), though the existence of a fourth for minor first aid treatment might be a useful addition. Further, there must be space for storing clean clothing and clean towels. Where the staffs include both sexes, two cleansing stations will be required.

Sketch plans of the lay-out for this accommodation are given in Figure 23. The following notes explain the requirements.

The shading shows portions in which gas vapour might collect.

External shed (or equivalent space indoors). This is needed for the removal of contaminated outer garments and boots. By this means the introduction of the grosser contamination into the building itself can be avoided. Where this space has to be provided within the building, the access to it should be unprotected by an air lock, and its windows should be kept open for constant ventilation. It should be treated as outside the gas-protected part of the building.

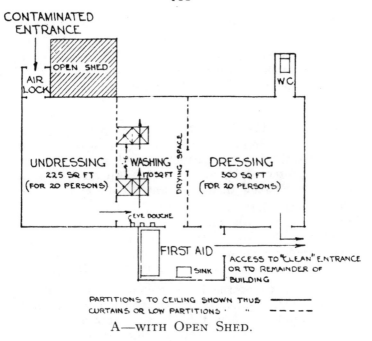

PARTITIONS TO CEILING SHOWN THUS ————
CURTAINS OR LOW PARTITIONS · " " — — — — —

A—WITH OPEN SHED.

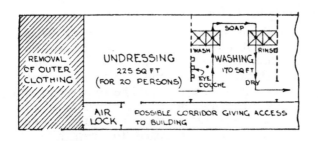

PARTITIONS TO CEILING SHOWN THUS ————
CURTAINS OR LOW PARTITIONS " " — — — — —

B— WITH ROOM IN PLACE OF OPEN SHED.

FIG. 23.—LAY-OUT OF CLEANSING DEPOT FOR
A.R.P. SERVICES.

There should be an air-lock between it and the rest of the building.

This space should be equipped with forms to sit on, preferably covered with american cloth, and it should contain bins with close fitting lids for contaminated clothing.

Room 1 (*Undressing*) should be as near as possible to the access from the shed or other space used for the removal of outer garments, and should in either case be protected by an air lock. An air lock is not necessary between this room and Room 2.

The undressing room should also be equipped with forms covered with american cloth, and bins for contaminated clothing. It should also have a latrine bucket, since men who are contaminated must not be allowed to use w.c.'s. which are used by other persons.

The capacity of the room should be assessed on a basis of about 15 sq. ft. per person. The size of the room should be such that it will accommodate the whole batch of men or women who might be expected to need it at one time, on the assumption that they would occupy it for about 5 minutes.

The washing arrangements in Room 2 should preferably consist of showers, with warm water. Four showers should be sufficient for a batch of 20 persons using the station at one time, but in large stations or depots more may be needed. The showers should preferably be arranged in two groups, with a space between, so that a man may wet himself under one shower, move into the space to soap himself, and then wash the soap off under a shower in the other group. Space in the washing room must be allowed for bleach treatment and eye treatment, if required in particular cases, and the men should dry themselves in this room (each being provided with a clean towel). It is suggested that a minimum space of 175 sq. ft. is required if only four showers are provided.

It should be a routine procedure to wash out the eyes freely in warm water.

When a separate first aid room is provided, it should be equipped with simple first aid requisites, and a trained attendant should be provided wherever possible.

Room 3 (*Dressing*), in which the men would change their clothing before going on duty as well as dressing after coming off duty, should have cupboards or lockers in which they could leave their own clothing, and in which *clean* protective clothing could be kept until required. In this room too about 15 sq. ft. should be allowed per person.

The cleansing station should be provided with its own staff, which should include, according to its size, two or more undressers (who must themselves wear respirators and protective clothing) and one attendant, or more, trained in giving bleach and eye treatment and minor first aid. The precise arrangements will vary with the service concerned.

The whole station (except a room provided in lieu of the open shed) should be gas-protected so that it could be used even if gas were present outside and should be as far as possible resistant to splinters and blast.

The contaminated entrance, past the open shed, should be reserved for this purpose, and should not be used for ordinary access into and out of the building for uncontaminated persons. There should be a bleach tray beside it in which each person entering should first wipe his boots. Rooms 1, 2 and 3 should, if possible, lead out of one another. Separate *rooms* are not essential, and it may often be necessary to divide up one or two large rooms to meet requirements. If a separate entrance and exit cannot be arranged in each room it is desirable to erect temporary barriers to avoid the possibility of contact between those entering and those coming out.

The average time required for dealing with contaminated persons after work may be reckoned at 25
minutes, made up as follows:—

	Minutes.
Undressing, including removal of anti-gas clothing	8
Washing and drying	7
Dressing	10

Notes on Design and Materials

The following notes apply to the undressing and
washing rooms, and to any room used instead of an
open shed.

The interior should be as simple in design as
possible, all unnecessary fittings, mouldings, etc., being
avoided so as to facilitate decontamination.

At least the lower portions of the rooms should be
constructed of smooth surfaced non-absorbent materials
which can be readily decontaminated. Adequate water
supply, and drainage facilities should be provided
whenever possible, to enable hosing down to be carried
out.

Each room should be capable of being well-
ventilated, so that it can be quickly cleared of any
concentration of gas which might collect in it; but
this problem (which should receive special attention
in cases where it is proposed to arrange cleansing
accommodation in the basement of the building) must,
of course, be considered in relation to the general
gasproofing arrangements in the building.

The recommendations as to materials given below
refer in particular to the use of materials in relation
to contamination by mustard gas, but may be taken
as being generally applicable to other types of blister
gas such as lewisite.

Floors. Flooring materials should be non-absorbent
to blister gas and be capable of decontamination by
the normal methods.

Generally the most suitable type of flooring is concrete with a granolithic or cement finish, both of which are improved by periodical treatment with a hardener such as sodium silicate solution. Proprietary waterproofing compounds, either pigmented or otherwise, may be used but have little effect on the behaviour of concrete towards mustard gas or decontamination processes. Acid-resisting or other special cements may be used but possess no special merit. Surface treatments of a bituminous nature are unsuitable for and increase the difficulties of decontamination.

Quarry tiles also provide a satisfactory flooring material. The tiles should be set in cement mortar with a fine joint and should also be periodically treated with sodium silicate solution. Unglazed tiles are not satisfactory, as the mustard gas is retained by the crazed surface.

In existing buildings the most satisfactory covering for wooden floors is sheet lead. This should be at least of 4 lbs. lead with burnt joints and be carried up the walls to form a coved skirting. A less expensive covering is linoleum (laid with as few joints as possible), but this has a comparatively short life under repeated decontamination.

Bare wooden floors, preferably of hardwood, may be used, but these are not recommended as repeated decontamination has an injurious effect on the timber. No advantage is gained by impregnating wooden floors with wood preservatives or fire-resisting compounds, and the use of varnish stains renders the process of decontamination more difficult.

Rubber flooring should not be used, as this material absorbs mustard gas.

Jointless flooring of the magnesium oxychloride type is unsuitable, as it is attacked by the solutions used in decontamination. Floorings of an asphaltic or bituminous nature are also unsuitable, since they absorb blister gas and are difficult to decontaminate. Such floorings should, therefore, be avoided in rooms where frequent decontamination might be necessary, but if in other situations an asphaltic flooring is desirable, a mixture containing the highest possible percentage of Trinidad Lake asphalt should be used.

Walls. As far as possible, walls, particularly the lower 6 ft., should be finished with smooth-surfaced impervious materials which can be washed and decontaminated.

The most satisfactory materials are glazed bricks or tiles which should be of the best quality in order to avoid crazing, and should be set in cement mortar with a fine joint.

Smooth Portland cement and sand forms a satisfactory finish and is improved by periodical treatment with sodium silicate solution. Plaster finishes of either lime plaster or gypsum (wall) plaster may also be used but must be similarly treated.

Corrugated galvanised sheets can be used, the sheets being fixed with the corrugations vertical, special care being taken with the joints.

Fair faced brickwork, where ordinary building bricks are used, is unsatisfactory.

Wall finishings of an asphaltic or bituminous nature should not be used as they absorb and retain mustard gas.

Wall linings and panelling of match-boarding, plywood, fibre board or asbestos cement sheeting are unsuitable unless all joints are covered and the whole finished with a varnished paper or a resistant paint coating to eliminate joints and porosity.

Mouldings and panelling should be avoided, and the angles between the walls and floor should be coved either with tiles or cement; wood skirting should be avoided.

Paintwork. Research is proceeding in connection with the development of a type of paint which will resist attack by blister gases and can be decontaminated without damage to the film. Ordinary paints are not satisfactory, and therefore the use of materials which require painting should be avoided as much as possible. Where woodwork, etc., has to be used, it should be painted with a hard-drying enamel paint, but it should be realised that under repeated contamination failure of the material must be anticipated.

Fittings. The number of fittings should be reduced to the minimum, and they should be of the simplest possible design with no unnecessary ornamentation. Essential fittings should where practicable be situated on the upper half of the walls so as to be out of the zone of heavier contamination. Doors should be of the flush type without moulding or panels, and metal windows should be provided.

Plastics of the phenol-formaldehyde or urea-formaldehyde type (e.g., Bakelite or Beatl or Scarab ware) are most suitable for fittings. The casein type of plastic is satisfactory but is water absorbent. Glazed porcelain is also satisfactory and metal pipes and fittings may be used but should be treated with a suitable paint to prevent corrosion by bleaching powder.

Oiled fabrics and american cloth may be used for covering wooden benches, etc., but they can only be decontaminated by means of boiling.

Hard ebonite materials are not recommended as they absorb mustard gas.

INDEX

I

THE EYES AND GAS

The eyes are always attacked by gas. As a preliminary treatment against the burning and irritation, it is well to advise the following :—

(1) That on no account should the eyes be rubbed, as this sets up further aggravation.

(2) A bottle of Optrex Eye Lotion should be readily available. This lotion, used with the special eye-bath, soothes the eyes and acts as a gentle antiseptic.

Optrex is recommended by Doctors and Opticians and may be used with complete confidence, pending further treatment. It is suitable for young and old alike.

Optrex
BRAND EYE LOTION

On sale at all Chemists at 2/- (with free eye-bath) Triple Size 3/6 (without eye-bath)

For interesting illustrated booklet "Sight—The Master Sense" full of vital information write to Wilcox Jozeau & Co., Ltd., Dept. A.P., North Circular Road, London, N.W.2.

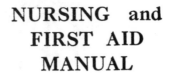

LIST OF MEMBERS OF
THE OILSKIN MANUFACTURERS'
ASSOCIATION OF GREAT BRITAIN

Abbett, Anderson & Abbott Ltd., Heathfield Works, Harpenden, Herts.

M. Barr & Co. Ltd., 28, Miller Street, Glasgow, C.1.

Chamberlins Ltd., Botolph Street Works, Norwich.

The Great Grimsby Coal, Salt & Tanning Co. Ltd., Fish Dock Road, Grimsby.

The Ioco Rubber & Waterproofing Co. Ltd., Netherton Works, Anniesland, Glasgow, W.3.

Johnson & Sons Ltd., Great Yarmouth.

Edward Macbean & Co. Ltd., Wellington Mills, Port Dundas, Glasgow, C.4.

H. E. Walters, Marlborough Road, Old Kent Road, London, S.E.1.

Official Publications on Air Raid Precautions

HANDBOOKS—
  See list on page ii within.

MEMORANDA—
  No. 1.—Organisation of Air Raid Casualties Services (*2nd edition*). 6d. (7d.)
  No. 2.—Rescue Parties and Clearance of Débris (*2nd edition*). 2d. (2½d.)
  No. 3.—Organisation of Decontamination Services (*2nd edition*). 2d. (2½d.)
  No. 4.—Air Raid Wardens (*1st edition*). 2d. (2½d.)
  No. 5.—Anti-Gas Training (*1st edition*). 4d. (5d.)
  No. 6.—Local Communications and Reporting of Air Raid Damage. (*in preparation*)
  No. 7.—Personnel Requirements for Air Raid General and Fire Precautions Services, and the Police Service (*1st edition*). 2d. (2½d.)

There is also a pamphlet on the Protection of Foodstuffs against Poison Gas (*1st edition*). 2d. (2½d.)

Prices are net, those in brackets include postage

H.M. STATIONERY OFFICE

LONDON, W.C.2   -   Adastral House, Kingsway
EDINBURGH 2   -   -   -   120 George Street
MANCHESTER 1   -   -   -   26 York Street
CARDIFF -   -   -   1 St. Andrew's Crescent
BELFAST -   -   -   80 Chichester Street
        or through any bookseller

S.O. Code No. 34–229–2–37

SOME THINGS YOU SHOULD KNOW IF WAR SHOULD COME

PUBLIC INFORMATION LEAFLET NO. 1

Read this and keep it carefully. **You may need it.**

Issued from the Lord Privy Seal's Office July, 1939

IF WAR SHOULD COME

The object of this leaflet is to tell you now some of the things you ought to know if you are to be ready for the emergency of war.

This does not mean that war is expected now, but it is everyone's duty to be prepared for the possibility of war.

Further leaflets will be sent to you to give you fuller guidance on particular ways in which you can be prepared.

The Government are taking all possible measures for the defence of the country, and have made plans for protecting you and helping you to protect yourselves, so far as may be, in the event of war.

You, in your turn, can help to make those plans work, if you understand them and act in accordance with them.

No-one can tell when or how war might begin, but the period of warning might be very short. There would be no time then to begin to think what you ought to do.

READ WHAT FOLLOWS, and think **NOW.**

---

(1) AIR RAID WARNINGS

When air raids are threatened, warning will be given in towns by sirens or hooters, which will be sounded, in some places by short blasts, and in other places by a warbling note, changing every few seconds. In war, sirens and hooters will not be used for any other purpose than this.

The warning may also be given by the Police or Air Raid Wardens blowing short blasts on whistles.

When you hear the warning, take cover at once. Remember that most of the injuries in an air raid are caused not by direct hits by bombs, but by flying fragments of debris or bits of shells. Stay under cover until you hear the sirens or hooters sounding continuously for two minutes on the same note, which is the signal " Raiders Passed."

If poison gas has been used, you will be warned by means of hand rattles. Keep off the streets until the poison gas has been cleared away. Hand bells will be rung when there is no longer any danger. If you hear the rattle when you are out, put on your gas mask at once and get indoors as soon as you can.

Make sure that all members of your household understand the meanings of these signals.

(2) GAS MASKS

If you have already got your gas mask, make sure that you are keeping it safely and in good condition for immediate use. If you are moving permanently, or going away for any length of time, remember to take your gas mask with you.

If you have not yet received your gas mask, the reason may be that it has been decided in your district to keep the masks in store until an emergency is threatened. If, however, you know that your neighbours have got their gas masks, and you have not got yours, report the matter to your Air Raid Warden.

The special anti-gas helmet for babies and the respirator for small children will not be distributed in any district before an emergency arises.

(3) LIGHTING RESTRICTIONS

All windows, sky-lights, glazed doors, or other openings which would show a light, will have to be screened in war time with dark blinds or blankets, or brown paper pasted on the glass, so that no light is visible from outside. You should obtain *now* any materials you may need for this purpose.

No outside lights will be allowed, and all street lighting will be put out.

Instructions will be issued about the dimming of lights on vehicles.

(4) FIRE PRECAUTIONS

An air attack may bring large numbers of small incendiary bombs, which might start so many fires that the Fire Brigades could not be expected to deal with them all. Everyone should be prepared to do all he can to tackle a fire started in his own house. Most large fires start as small ones.

Clearing the top floor of all inflammable materials, lumber, etc., will lessen the danger of fire, and prevent a fire from spreading. See that you can reach your attic or roof space readily.

Water is the best means of putting out a fire started by an incendiary bomb. Have some buckets handy. But water can only be applied to the bomb itself in the form of a fine spray, for which a handpump with a length of hose and special nozzle are needed. **If you throw a bucket of water on a burning incendiary bomb it will explode and throw burning fragments in all directions.** You may be able to smother it with sand or dry earth.

(5) EVACUATION

Arrangements have been made by the Government for the voluntary evacuation from certain parts of the London area and of some other large towns of schoolchildren, children below school age if accompanied by their mothers or other responsible persons, expectant mothers, and adult blind persons who can be moved.

Parents in the districts concerned who wish to take advantage of the Government evacuation scheme for their children have already received or will receive full instructions what to do, if the need arises.

Those who have already made, or are making arrangements to send their children away to relations or friends must remember that while the Government evacuation scheme is in progress, ordinary railway and road services will necessarily be drastically reduced and subject to alterations at short notice.

Try to decide now whether you wish your children to go under the Government evacuation scheme and let your local authority know : if you propose to make private arrangements to send your children away do not leave them to the last moment.

All who have work to do, whether manual, clerical or professional, should regard it as their duty to remain at their posts, and do their part in carrying on the life of the nation.

(6) IDENTITY LABELS

In war you should carry about with you your name and address clearly written. This should be on an envelope, card or luggage label, *not* on some odd piece of paper easily lost. In the case of children a label should be fastened, e.g. sewn, on to their clothes, in such a way that it will not readily become detached.

(7) FOOD

It is very important that at the outset of an emergency people should not buy larger quantities of foodstuffs than they normally buy and normally require. The Government are making arrangements to ensure that there will be sufficient supplies of food, and that every person will be able to obtain regularly his or her fair share ; and they will take steps to prevent any sudden rise in prices. But if some people try to buy abnormal quantities, before the full scheme of control is working, they will be taking food which should be available for others.

If you wish, and are able to lay in a small extra store of non-perishable foodstuffs, there is no reason why you should not do so. They will be an additional insurance. But you should collect them now and not when an emergency arises.

(8) INSTRUCTIONS TO THE PUBLIC IN CASE OF EMERGENCY.

Arrangements will be made for information and instructions to be issued to the public in case of emergency, both through the Press, and by means of Broadcast Announcements. Broadcasts may be made at special times, which will be announced beforehand, or during the ordinary News Bulletins.

YOUR GAS MASK

**How to keep it
and How to Use it**

—

MASKING YOUR
WINDOWS

—

PUBLIC INFORMATION
LEAFLET NO. 2

Read   this   and
keep   it   carefully.
You may need it.

Issued from the Lord Privy Seal's Office July, 1939

YOUR GAS MASK

TAKE CARE OF YOUR GAS MASK AND YOUR GAS MASK WILL TAKE CARE OF YOU. It is possible that in war your life might depend on your gas mask and the condition in which it had been kept.

The official gas mask, or respirator, consists of a metal container filled with material which absorbs the gas, and a rubber facepiece with a non-inflammable transparent window. Some people seem to think that this mask does not look as if it would offer very good protection. Actually, it has been most carefully designed and fully tested, and will give you adequate protection against breathing any of the known war gases. But remember it will not protect you from the ordinary gas that you burn in a gas cooker or gas fire.

HOW TO STORE IT

Your mask should be kept carefully. Never hang it up by the straps which fasten it on over the head. This will pull the rubber facepiece out of shape so that it no longer fits you properly. It should be kept in the special box provided, where this has been issued, but any box which is air tight, or nearly so, will do.

When placed in the box the metal container should lie flat with the rubber facepiece uppermost, the transparent window lying evenly on top at full length. Great care should be taken not to bend or fold the window, or to let it get scratched, cracked or dented.

Keep the box in a cool place away from strong light. Exposure to heat or prolonged exposure to strong light will spoil the material of the mask and it may cease to give complete protection. It should never be held close to a fire or hot water pipes, or left lying out in the sun.

HOW TO PUT IT ON AND TAKE IT OFF

It is important to know how to put on your mask quickly and properly. You might need to do this in a hurry. To put it on, hold the mask by each of the side straps with the thumbs underneath and the inside of the window facing you. Then lift the mask to your face, push your chin forwards into it and draw the straps over the top of your head as far as they will go. See that the straps are properly adjusted and leave them so.

To remove the mask, insert the thumb under the buckle at the back of your head and then pull it forward over the top of your head so that the mask is lowered downwards from the face.

*NEVER TRY TO LIFT THE MASK OFF UPWARDS OR
BY PULLING THE CONTAINER OR THE EDGE OF THE
RUBBER AT THE CHIN.*

To prevent the window from misting over when the mask is worn, wet the end of a finger and rub it on a piece of toilet soap. Then rub the finger all over the inside of the window so as to leave a thin film of soap.

PUTTING YOUR MASK AWAY

After the mask has been used you will find that it is wet on the inside with moisture from the breath. This should be wiped off with a soft dry cloth and the mask allowed to dry before it is put away in its box. Do not try to dry it by applying heat.

The contents of the container do not deteriorate either with age or with wearing the mask when gas is not present. But if you suspect any flaw in your gas mask you should inform your local air raid warden.

It is a good thing to get out your gas mask occasionally and put it on, so as to get used to wearing it, and if you take the simple precautions set out above you will ensure that it is always ready for your protection.

MASKING YOUR WINDOWS

In war, one of our great protections against the dangers of air attack after nightfall would be the " black-out." On the outbreak of hostilities all external lights and street lighting would be totally extinguished so as to give hostile aircraft no indication as to their whereabouts. But this will not be fully effective unless *you* do your part, and see to it that no lighting in the house where you live is visible from the outside. The motto for safety will be " Keep it dark ! "

Every occupier of rooms, house or flat would be responsible for darkening his own lights. Lights in the halls or on the staircases of blocks of flats or dwellings would be the responsibility of the landlord or owner.

Of course, the most convenient way of shutting in the light is to use close fitting blinds. These can be of any thick, dark coloured material such as dark blue or black or dark green glazed Holland, Lancaster or Italian Cloth.

If you cannot manage this, you could obscure your windows by fixing up sheets of black paper or thick dark brown paper mounted on battens.

Alternatively, thick curtains of suitable material will serve, if they really cover the window frames with a bit to spare all round.

The simplest way of testing material, whether for blinds or curtains, is to hold up a piece against an electric bulb. If no light shows through, or only scattered pin holes of light are seen, then the material will do. If a patch of light shows through, it is no use.

Possibly you have blinds already fitted to your windows. If the material is not sufficiently opaque, you can treat it with Oil Bound Water Paint or Distemper of some dark colour. The following mixture can be applied with a brush :—

1 lb. of concentrated size, 3 lb. lamp black in powder form, $\frac{1}{2}$ gill of gold size. The size and lamp black should be thoroughly mixed and $2\frac{1}{2}$ gallons of boiling water added. This quantity will cover about 80 square yards of material.

If your blinds do not fit very closely, you could paint the edges of the window panes all round with dark paint. It will, of course, help if you also shade your lights so as to prevent any light falling directly on the window.

Most Important—do not forget your skylight if you have one, or glazed doors or even fanlights. You may find it simplest to make these permanently obscure by applying sufficient coats of some dark distemper or paint, or pasting them over with thick brown paper.

There is another thing to remember—Make sure that no light shows when your front door or back door is open. In some cases it may be possible to fix a curtain in the hall or passage to form a " light lock," but if this cannot be done, the light must be turned off before the door is opened.

Some people perhaps will only use one or two rooms at night in war time. This, of course, would simplify matters considerably, as the precautions indicated would only have to be taken for those particular rooms. But you would have to take care not to show by mistake any light in a room where the windows were not screened, and also to see that light did not reach the window of an unoccupied room through some open door.

Do not leave things until the last, but get together the materials which you think you would need. If you wait, you might find that you had difficulty in getting what you wanted. Besides, your help is wanted in making effective the " black-outs " for the A.R.P. exercises which are being arranged to try out our defences from time to time.

After all, it is only common sense to make our preparations in advance to meet a possible emergency.

EVACUATION
WHY AND HOW?

PUBLIC INFORMATION
LEAFLET   NO. 3

Read   this   and
keep   it   carefully.
You   may   need   it.

Issued from the Lord Privy Seal's Office July, 1939

WHY EVACUATION?

There are still a number of people who ask " What is the need for all this business about evacuation ? Surely if war comes it would be better for families to stick together and not go breaking up their homes ? "

It is quite easy to understand this feeling, because it is difficult for us in this country to realise what war in these days might mean. If we were involved in war, our big cities might be subjected to determined attacks from the air—at any rate in the early stages—and although our defences are strong and are rapidly growing stronger, some bombers would undoubtedly get through.

We must see to it then that the enemy does not secure his chief objects—the creation of anything like panic, or the crippling dislocation of our civil life.

One of the first measures we can take to prevent this is the removal of the children from the more dangerous areas.

THE GOVERNMENT EVACUATION SCHEME

The Government have accordingly made plans for the removal from what are called " evacuable " areas (see list at the back of this leaflet) to safer places called " reception " areas, of school children, children below school age if accompanied by their mothers or other responsible persons, and expectant mothers and blind persons.

The scheme is entirely a voluntary one, but clearly the children will be much safer and happier away from the big cities where the dangers will be greatest.

There is room in the safer areas for these children; householders have volunteered to provide it. They have offered homes where the children will be made welcome. The children will have their schoolteachers and other helpers with them and their schooling will be continued.

WHAT YOU HAVE TO DO

Schoolchildren

Schoolchildren would assemble at their schools when told to do so and would travel together with their teachers by train. The transport of some 3,000,000 in all is an enormous undertaking. *It would not be possible to let all parents know in advance the place to which each child is to be sent but they would be notified as soon as the movement is over.*

If you have children of school age, you have probably already heard from the school or the local education authority the necessary details of what you would have to do to get your child or children taken away. *Do not hesitate to register your children under this scheme, particularly if you are living in a crowded area.* Of course it means heartache to be separated from your children, but you can be quite sure that they will be well looked after. That will relieve you of one anxiety at any rate. You cannot wish, if it is possible to evacuate them, to let your children experience the dangers and fears of air attack in crowded cities.

Children under five

Children below school age must be accompanied by their mothers or some other responsible person. Mothers who wish to go away with such children should register with the Local Authority. *Do not delay in making enquiries about this.*

A number of mothers in certain areas have shown reluctance to register. Naturally, they are anxious to stay by their menfolk. Possibly they are thinking that they might as well wait and see; that it may not be so bad after all. *Think this over carefully and think of your child or children in good time.* Once air attacks have begun it might be very difficult to arrange to get away.

Expectant Mothers

Expectant mothers can register at any maternity or child welfare centre. For any further information inquire at your Town Hall.

The Blind

In the case of the Blind, registration to come under the scheme can be secured through the home visitors, or enquiry may be made at the Town Hall.

PRIVATE ARRANGEMENTS

If you have made private arrangements for getting away your children to relatives or friends in the country, or intend to make them, you should remember that while the Government evacuation scheme is in progress ordinary railway and road services will necessarily be drastically reduced and subject to alteration at short notice. Do not, therefore, in an emergency leave your private plans to be carried out at the last moment. It may then be too late.

If you happen to be away on holiday in the country or at the seaside and an emergency arises, do not attempt to take your children back home if you live in an " evacuable " area.

WORK MUST GO ON

The purpose of evacuation is to remove from the crowded and vulnerable centres, if an emergency should arise, those, more particularly the children, whose presence cannot be of any assistance.

Everyone will realise that there can be no question of wholesale clearance. We are not going to win a war by running away.

Most of us will have work to do, and work that matters, because we must maintain the nation's life and the production of munitions and other material essential to our war effort. For most of us therefore, who do not go off into the Fighting Forces our duty will be to stand by our jobs or those new jobs which we may undertake in war.

Some people have asked what they ought to do if they have no such definite work or duty.

You should be very sure before deciding that there is really nothing you can do. There is opportunity for a vast variety of services in civil defence. YOU must judge whether in fact you can or cannot help by remaining. If you are sure you cannot, then there is every reason why you should go away if you can arrange to do so, but you should take care to avoid interfering with the official evacuation plans. If you are proposing to use the public transport services, make your move either BEFORE the evacuation of the children begins or AFTER it has been completed. You will not be allowed to use transport required for the official evacuation scheme and other essential purposes, and you must not try to take accommodation which is required for the children and mothers under the Government scheme.

For the rest, we must remember that it would be essential that the work of the country should go on. Men and women alike will have to stand firm, to maintain our effort for victory. Such measures of protection as are possible are being pushed forward for the large numbers who have to remain at their posts. That they will be ready to do so, no one doubts.

The " evacuable " areas under the Government scheme are:—

(*a*) London, as well as the County Boroughs of West Ham and East Ham; the Boroughs of Walthamstow, Leyton, Ilford and Barking in Essex; the Boroughs of Tottenham, Hornsey, Willesden, Acton, and Edmonton in Middlesex; (*b*) the Medway towns of Chatham, Gillingham and Rochester; (*c*) Portsmouth, Gosport and Southampton; (*d*) Birmingham and Smethwick; (*e*) Liverpool, Bootle, Birkenhead and Wallasey; (*f*) Manchester and Salford; (*g*) Sheffield, Leeds, Bradford and Hull; (*h*) Newcastle and Gateshead; (*i*) Edinburgh, Rosyth, Glasgow, Clydebank and Dundee.

In some of these places only certain areas will be evacuated. Evacuation may be effected from a few other places in addition to the above, of which notice will be given.

YOUR FOOD IN WAR-TIME

PUBLIC INFORMATION LEAFLET NO. 4

Read this and
keep it carefully.
You may need it.

Issued from the Lord Privy Seal's Office July, 1939

YOUR FOOD IN WAR-TIME

You know that our country is dependent to a very large extent on supplies of food from overseas. More than 20 million tons are brought into our ports from all parts of the world in the course of a year. Our defence plans must therefore provide for the protection of our trade routes by which these supplies reach us, for reserves of food here and for the fair distribution of supplies, both home and imported, as they become available.

WHAT THE GOVERNMENT HAVE DONE

During the last eighteen months the Government have purchased considerable reserves of essential foodstuffs which are additional to the commercial stocks normally carried. This is one of the precautionary measures which has been taken to build up our resources to meet the conditions of war. In addition, the necessary arrangements have been made to control the supply and distribution of food throughout the country immediately upon the outbreak of hostilities and to bring in such measure of rationing as may be required.

HOW YOU CAN HELP

There are certain ways in which traders and householders can help to strengthen our food position at the present time.

In the ordinary way, the stocks of food in any area are based on the extent of the local demand, or the size of the local population. In war time, the amount of stocks in any area might be affected by air raid damage, or the flow of supplies might be reduced temporarily by transport difficulties.

As an additional precaution against difficulties of this kind, traders will be doing a good service *now* by maintaining, and if possible increasing, their stocks, so far as they can. You, too, as an ordinary householder, will be doing a good service if you can manage to get in some extra stores of food that will keep. These will be a stand-by against an emergency. Of course, there are many of us who cannot do this, but those who can will find, if a strain is put at any time upon local supplies, that such reserves will not only be a convenience to themselves but will help their neighbours. By drawing on these reserves instead of making demands on the shops at such a time, they would leave the stocks available for the use of those who have not been able to put anything by.

For those who have the means, a suitable amount of foodstuffs to lay by would be the quantity that they ordinarily use in one week. The following are suggested as articles of food suitable for householder's storage:—

Meat and fish in cans or glass jars; flour; suet; canned or dried milk; sugar; tea; cocoa; plain biscuits.

When you have laid in your store, you should draw on it regularly for day to day use, replacing what you use by new purchases, so that the stock in your cupboard is constantly being changed. Flour and suet in particular should be replaced frequently. You may find it helpful to label the articles with the date of purchase.

Any such reserves should be bought before an emergency arises. To try to buy extra quantities when an emergency is upon us, would be unfair to others.

FOOD SUPPLIES FOR EVACUATION

The Government evacuation scheme, of which you have already been told, will mean a considerable shift of population from the more vulnerable areas to safer areas. This will lead to additional demands on shops in the reception areas. Traders have been asked to have plans in readiness for increasing the supplies in shops in reception areas to meet the needs of the increased population. It would, however, take a day or two for these plans to be put into full operation.

The Government are, therefore, providing emergency supplies for children and others travelling under the official evacuation scheme. These supplies would be issued to them on their arrival in their new areas and would be sufficient for two days. Those who receive them will be asked not to make any purchases, other than small ones, in the local shops during those two days.

Those making their own arrangements to travel, should take food with them sufficient for two days, and should buy in advance, as part of their arrangements, the non-perishable food which they would require. As already said, anyone who, in time of emergency, buys more than normal quantities, would be doing harm, as such buying must draw on stocks which should be available for others.

NATIONAL HOUSEKEEPING IN WAR TIME
CENTRAL CONTROL

Should war come, the Government would take over responsibility for obtaining the main food supplies for the country, and for distributing them through all the stages down to the consumer. This would ensure that every precaution could be taken against war time risks. The prices of food would be controlled and supplies directed wherever they were needed.

For this purpose, the existing organisation of the food trades would be used so far as possible, and all food traders—importers, manufacturers, wholesalers and retailers—would work under the direction of a Ministry of Food. The Ministry would act for the benefit of the country as a whole and be assisted by representatives of the various trades.

LOCAL DISTRIBUTION

In each area food control would be in the hands of a local committee, which would be set up at the outbreak of war. The membership of these committees would be chosen to represent the general body of consumers in the area. It would include a few retail traders who possess a first-hand working knowledge of trading conditions.

The principal duty of these local Food Control Committees would be to look after the interests of consumers. They will also be responsible for supervising retail distribution. Shopkeepers would be licensed to trade by these committees. Ordinarily, all existing shops would receive these licences. New shops would not be opened unless there was a need for them.

Shopkeepers would be instructed that they must not supply excessive quantities to any of their customers, and powers would be taken to prevent people from buying more than their reasonable share.

Maximum prices would be fixed by the Ministry for each controlled food, and would be shown clearly in the shop windows.

RATIONING SCHEME

Certain foods, soon after the outbreak of a war, would be brought under a rationing scheme similar to that which was introduced during the latter part of the Great War. In the first instance, rationing would be applied to five foodstuffs—butcher's meat, bacon and ham, sugar, butter and margarine, and cooking fats. Later, it might be necessary to add other articles.

The object of this scheme is to make certain that foodstuffs are distributed fairly and equally and that everyone is sure of his or her proper share.

Before rationing begins application forms would be sent through the post to every householder, who would be asked to give particulars of everyone living in his home. These forms, when filled in, would be returned to the local food office set up by the local Food Control Committee, which would issue the Ration Books, one for each person.

You would then register at a retail shop of your own choice for each rationed food. This registration is necessary to enable the local committee to know the quantities of rationed foods which each shop would require. There is no need to register with a shop in peace time. It is not advisable to do so.

The Ration Books would have coupons, a certain number for each week. The Ministry would decide how much food each coupon represented, and you would be entitled to buy that amount. In the case of meat, the amount would be expressed in money. Thus, you could choose between buying a larger amount of a cheaper cut, or a smaller amount of a more expensive cut. In the case of other foods, the amount would be by weight.

For children under six years of age, there would be a Child's Ration Book, but the only difference would be that a child would be allowed half the amount of butcher's meat allowed for a grown-up person. On the other hand, the allowance for a heavy worker will give him a larger quantity of meat.

For catering and other institutions, special arrangements will be made.

These are the plans for our national housekeeping in war time. Like all plans for our civil defence they need your help. In war time there would be no food to waste, but with your care and co-operation we shall have enough.

Any enquiries about food supplies in war time should be addressed:— The Director, Food (Defence Plans) Department, Great Westminster House, Horseferry Road. London, S.W.1.

ORGANIZATION OF THE AIR RAID WARDENS' SERVICE

CONTENTS

ORGANISATION OF THE AIR RAID WARDENS' SERVICE

Introduction

The Duties of Air Raid Wardens have been described in Air Raid Precautions Handbook No. 8. This Memorandum is concerned with the organisation to be established by local authorities for the provision of a Wardens' Service, in accordance with paragraph 4 of the Schedule to the Air Raid Precautions (General Schemes) Regulations, 1938.

The wardens will be needed to perform a number of important duties in case of air attack, and thereby to augment and relieve the normal resources of the civil authorities for safeguarding the general public. Their work as wardens will in the normal case be undertaken close to their homes or places of work. They will constitute an essential part of the air raid precautions services to be provided by local authorities.

Their chief duties in time of peace will be to establish contact with their fellow-citizens in their sectors, and to advise them on the officially recommended precautions against air raids. In time of war, they will have to be at their posts as required, to report immediately the particulars of air raid damage, to know how to begin relief measures, and generally to assist the inhabitants of their sectors.

In addition wardens have an important part to play in connection with the provision of respirators for the general public. This aspect of their duties has been dealt with in separate communications to local authorities.

PART I.—GENERAL

1. The Purpose of Air Raid Wardens

The intention is that an air raid warden will be a responsible member of the public chosen to be a leader and adviser of his neighbours in a small area or '' sector ''—a street or a small group of streets—in which he is known and respected. It is not contemplated that wardens will normally be used outside the immediate neighbourhood of their homes or places of business.

A

Apart from their general duty to aid and advise their neighbours and to see that they are provided with respirators, air raid wardens can be of great value to supplement the resources of the police, the fire brigade, and the other local air raid precautions services, in various ways, for instance:—

(a) by helping to shepherd members of the public to shelter when an air raid warning is received, and assisting to deal with casualties or damage after bombs have fallen, until skilled help arrives;

(b) by affording a channel by which the responsible officials can be rapidly informed of the fall of bombs in any part of the district, and of the extent of the damage caused;

(c) by giving immediate warning in their locality of the presence or suspected presence of gas; and

(d) most of all, by setting an example of coolness and steadiness among their neighbours, and so reducing the risk of panic and loss of morale.

2. Scheme of Organisation

Control by Chief Constables

The effective performance of the duties of air raid wardens depends more on the personality and standing of the wardens themselves than on any powers in law. Police powers, for instance, are not essential.* Air raid wardens should be looked upon as a separate corps, not forming part of the police or special constabulary, even though organised under the Chief Officer of Police.

The functions of air raid wardens are, however, allied to those of the police, and the public ought to look to them for responsible help and guidance in the same way that it is accustomed to look to the police. Further, in time of war the wardens would be closely associated with the police in their work of maintaining public order. These considerations have led many local authorities to entrust to the Chief Constable the executive work in connection with the wardens' service. This course has been followed not only in boroughs having separate police forces, but also in a number of county areas.

It should in future be the normal arrangement (outside the Metropolitan Police District) for the responsibility for framing

---

* A warden would have the right, which is possessed by every citizen, to arrest any person who is committing, or has committed, a treason or felony, as also to prevent a breach of the peace which is taking place, or is about to take place, or on a " hue and cry," i.e., in the immediate pursuit of a felon etc. This power could for instance be used in a case of looting.

the organisation of the wardens' service in peace time, as well as for exercising control in time of war, to be entrusted to the Chief Constable, in counties and boroughs alike. The duties falling on the police in connection with an emergency are, however, substantial, and are very greatly increased in time of war: the additional work of controlling the wardens' service, if it is organised under the Chief Constable, will be more than can be borne by the ordinary administrative organisation of the police force. The Chief Constable, or the senior police officer in the area, would have control, but he would require (in addition to a Chief Warden) a special office staff to do the detailed work under him.

It may be possible for some members of the special constabulary whose services are not likely to be required for duty as special constables to enrol also as air raid wardens, on the understanding that if employed in the latter capacity they would not be regarded as on special constabulary duty.

Alternative systems of control already adopted

In some areas the wardens' service may have been organised independently of the police, under the control of some chief officer of the council and not of the Chief Constable. On this system the Chief Warden is in direct executive charge, but is responsible to the permanent officer deputed to exercise supervision and control.

In other areas the service may have been framed on the basis that in time of war the wardens would operate under the control of the Chief Constable: but in time of peace they have been organised under a Chief Warden, appointed by the local authority concerned in consultation with the Chief Constable, the Chief Warden being responsible for the recruitment and training of wardens with such assistance from the police as may be arranged.

While it should in future be the normal arrangement for the wardens' service to be organised by and under the control of the Chief Constable, the institution of this arrangement may be deferred in any area, with the concurrence of the Air Raid Precautions Department, if the Department is satisfied on representations by the local authority that either of the other two systems noted above has been instituted and is operating satisfactorily in the area and that there are circumstances which make it inappropriate to change the system at the moment.

PART II.—DESCRIPTION OF THE WARDENS' SERVICE

3. Wardens' Posts

The unit of organisation for the wardens' service in war is the wardens' post, which should serve one or more sectors, each comprising a resident population of about 500. For the purpose of the demarcation of these sectors the first consideration is the resident population, but there may be other factors to be taken into account.

The wardens' post is the place at which the wardens allotted to the sector or sectors served by the post would assemble on the air raid warning. It should be in a prominent position, both from the point of view of giving good observation to the warden on look-out and also of being easily found by members of the public. Wardens will make their reports of damage or other incidents in the sectors from the post, which will therefore need a telephone.

The post should be large enough to provide room for the storage in war of the protective clothing and other gear of the wardens belonging to the sectors which the post serves, and should be capable of affording protection for the wardens against the blast and splinters of high explosive bombs.

Spacing of Wardens' Posts

In the original concept of the wardens' organisation it was contemplated that there should be a warden's post in every sector. Examination of the problem of providing and maintaining telephone service for wardens posts has, however, made it necessary to revise this arrangement. In time of war the maintenance of the telephone services for reporting by wardens might become a matter of difficulty and in order to secure an efficient service for essential telephones it might be necessary to impose severe restrictions on the use of telephones generally. The problem has therefore become one of determining to what extent the telephone facilities for the wardens' organisation can be reduced without detracting from the efficiency of the reporting services.

It is considered that in densely populated areas it would be sufficient if there were a wardens' post with telephone facilities every 500 or 600 yards. Local authorities have already in practically all cases planned out their areas in wardens' sectors on the present basis of about 500 inhabitants to a sector and this layout can be retained but sectors can be combined so that two or three or more sectors can be worked from a common post.

The principles on which wardens' posts should now be chosen should therefore be that in no case should posts be spaced more closely than one per sector, and in areas where the size of sectors is small, posts should nowhere be closer together than ¼ mile measured in a straight line on the map and may well be farther apart, provided that no fully built-up part of the sectors which they serve should be more than $\frac{1}{4}$ mile from the post measured by the shortest route available for a warden to proceed on foot. It is considered that a maximum of about 10 posts to the square mile should be sufficient to meet requirements in fully built-up and densely populated areas, it being understood that in the less densely populated parts and on the outskirts of towns the spacing of posts would be more sparse.

The local authority, having determined the number of posts and their location on the principles laid down above, should proceed to select the premises to be used for the purpose. In many cases, a building such as a school, a hall, or a garage, will obviously afford the best location. In others it may be more convenient to use the house of one of the wardens, or his shop, if he is willing. In all cases full arrangements for their immediate occupation in an emergency should be made.

It may not be practicable to find adequate premises immediately for all the posts required, but urgent steps should be taken to secure the necessary premises for at least three posts in each group of sectors under a Head Warden, and these posts should have telephones installed ready for emergency.

Numbers of Wardens

The number of wardens who may be enrolled on the war establishment of each local authority has been laid down by the Air Raid Precautions Department, on the general basis of six wardens per 500 population in important urban areas, and lower proportions for other areas. These will be allotted by the local authority to sectors, proportionately to their size and importance, and the number of wardens available for the manning of any particular post will depend on the numbers allotted to the sector or sectors which that post serves.

Two wardens in each sector should be appointed as Senior Warden and Second Warden respectively to have charge of the wardens in the sector. Where one post serves several sectors steps should be taken to make clear which of the senior or second wardens on duty at any one time is to have charge of the working of the post.

It is very desirable that wherever possible additional persons should be enrolled and trained beyond the actual requirements of the number of posts to be manned, in order to provide a reserve to be called upon in case of need.

Where there are large blocks of flats or tenements with more than, say, 100 residents, it is recommended that special wardens should be appointed for each block (chosen from those living or employed in the premises where possible), and as these wardens could be of assistance to the wardens in the post in the street, the sector worked from the street post could, in such circumstances, contain more than 500 residents. The wardens in the flats or tenements should normally be regarded as part of the public wardens' service, and should be appointed and trained by the local authority.

In business and industrial premises containing more than, say, 100 employees, the owners or occupiers should be encouraged to organise factory guards or office guards for duty within the premises. The factory guards or office guards would not be part of the public wardens' service, but the sectors of the public wardens in the streets in these areas should contain substantially more than 500 occupants of the buildings.

While the factory guards and office guards organised by occupiers of large factories and offices should not, as such, form part of the public wardens' service, the same people can quite well be enrolled as public wardens for duty outside their working hours in their home localities.

Numbers in Country Districts

The numbers of wardens allotted to rural areas are on the basis of about three wardens per 500 population. Their sectors will normally be whole villages or parishes, the number of wardens for each depending on the population. One post in the village or parish, used as a rallying point for air raid precautions volunteers generally, will then be sufficient, and individual wardens could operate mainly from their own homes. Since the wardens and their homes will be well known to everyone in a small community, this arrangement will be convenient because the wardens will thus be spread over the area.

4. The Organisation of the Wardens' Service

The executive head of the wardens' service in each area* should be a Chief Warden, who will require a deputy. The selection of suitable persons for these positions is a matter of great importance.

The Chief Warden, and the Head Wardens and Divisional Wardens described below, will not be paid officials but will be volunteers, as are other members of the wardens' service.

The number of subordinates whom the Chief Warden will require will depend on the total number of wardens under his control. It is suggested that posts may suitably be organised in Groups covering a population of from 6,000 to 10,000, or more in densely populated areas, each under a Head Warden. In counties and the larger towns, it may be convenient to organise Groups of posts in Divisions, each under a Divisional

---

* *Note.*—It is a matter for consideration in the larger counties whether there is need for a County Chief Warden, even if the wardens' service is one service for the whole county. It may be found better to have separate Chief Wardens for different parts of the county—e.g., for police divisions or other convenient areas.

Warden, in order to form a suitable chain of control between the Chief Warden and the Head Wardens. The structure of the organisation might thus be, for a town of 100,000 inhabitants—

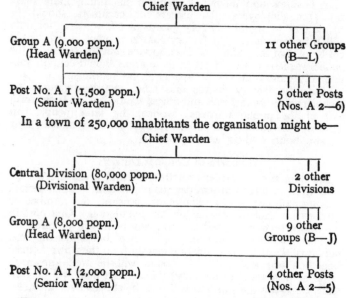

In a town of 250,000 inhabitants the organisation might be—

The organisation in county areas will be on similar lines, depending perhaps on the size of police divisions, or on the size of the area selected for the formation of a separate wardens' organisation under a Chief Warden.

Each group of sectors and posts should be distinguished by a letter. The posts belonging to the group will be indicated by that letter coupled with a number—thus one group of sectors and posts would be Group A and the posts in the group would be numbered A1, A2, A3 and so on. It is preferable, for purposes of reporting in war, that the numbering series A1, A2, etc., should be the numbers of the *posts,* not of the sectors, which should be otherwise distinguished—e.g., where more than one sector is attached to post A1, the sectors might be known as sectors A1 (*a*), A1 (*b*), etc.

Where the wardens, in the area of any one Chief Warden, are organised in more than four Groups it is desirable that there should be, as a paid appointment, an officer whose principal duty it would be to foster the efficiency of the wardens' service, in addition to taking charge of the routine duties of training and organisation. If the Chief Constable is in executive charge of the service he will probably make this appointment from among the responsible officers of his force. In other cases local authorities should consider such an appointment and should be careful to choose a person whose keenness and character will encourage the wardens. The officer should act as Chief Assistant to the Chief Warden in matters of organisation and, in areas large enough to have the wardens' Groups organised in Divisions, a similar Divisional Assistant might be appointed to assist the Divisional Warden. The Assistant should be provided with such clerical assistance as is required for maintaining proper records, etc.

The Head Warden, Divisional Warden and Chief Warden should take part in arranging the recruitment and training of wardens, and would be responsible for allotting them to posts, and arranging rotas of duty, replacement in cases of sickness or injury, and so on. They would not however constitute a chain of communication in time of air raids: the individual wardens would send their reports direct in accordance with the local instructions and not through their Head Warden or Divisional Warden.

5. Equipment of Wardens' Posts

The following articles will be supplied by the Government for every six wardens on the establishment approved in the local scheme:—

6 armlets (of standard design).
6 steel helmets.
6 Civilian Duty respirators.
3 light oilskin anti-gas suits.
3 pairs rubber boots.
3 pairs anti-gas gloves.
6 anti-gas eye shields.
3 anti-gas curtains.

together with reserve quantities as necessary.

The following articles will also be required at each post. They are to be supplied by local authorities on grant-aided terms, but arrangements for their purchase under bulk contracts placed by the Government are available for any local authority wishing to take advantage of them. The numbers quoted show the approximate quantities required for every six wardens:—

A manuscript book for recording occurrences.
3 electric torches.
3 whistles.
2 hand rattles.
1 hand bell.
Small first aid box.

Local authorities will be given an opportunity to obtain on a grant aided basis stirrup hand pumps for supply to some at any rate of the wardens' posts in their areas.

Except for the armlet and steel helmet, all this equipment (including the respirators, etc.) will be kept at the post, and not be taken home by the individual wardens. They will have Civilian respirators, like everyone else, for use when not on duty.

It should not be necessary to supply individual wardens with large scale maps of their sectors: the individual sector is very small, and they should be sufficiently familiar with the locality not to need a map. It may however be convenient to supply Head Wardens and Divisional Wardens with maps of the area for which they are responsible. In towns these might need to be on the 6 inch scale, but in country areas the 1 inch scale would normally be suitable.

Cleansing facilities will not be provided in wardens' posts. In the event of wardens becoming contaminated with blister gas, they should go to a First Aid Post for cleansing.

PART III.—ENROLMENT OF WARDENS

6. Qualifications of Wardens

Air raid wardens should be men, generally over 30 years of age, or women.

They should be of good character, level-headed, and free from obvious physical or temperamental disability. On general grounds, the older men and women with a good sense of responsibility and of a type to inspire confidence among their neighbours, will be most suitable.

It will be of great advantage if the wardens live near the posts they are to man, so that every locality should so far as possible be self-contained in this respect. Similarly posts in business and industrial areas should be manned, for raids during working hours, by wardens who work nearby.

No one should be enrolled who is a member of the Territorial Army or the Auxiliary Air Force, or is liable to recall as a reservist to the Defence Forces, or has undertaken to join a police force or fire brigade for emergency service (as to special constabulary service, see Section 2).

7. Card of Appointment for Wardens

Wardens should be provided with a card of appointment as evidence of their *bona fides* in their dealings with householders in their sectors. An A.R.P. Badge is not evidence of authority to act as a warden.

A suggested form of card, which should be signed by the Clerk to the local authority, or by the Chief Constable, is given below.

Name of Local Authority

Air Raid Precautions

This is to certify that [*name and address of warden*] has been duly appointed as an air raid warden. This is his authority to carry out the duties laid upon wardens by the [County Council] [*or* Chief Constable].

Signed ....
[Clerk *or* Chief Constable.]

Date of issue of card ....

Date of appointment of warden ....

Signature of warden ....

PART IV.—TRAINING OF WARDENS

8. Individual and collective training

In common with the other air raid precautions services an air raid warden's training must include precautions against gas. A revised and shortened syllabus for a full anti-gas course (of about 9 hours) which will be applicable to air raid wardens and other outdoor services has been prepared and will be communicated to local authorities very shortly.

The training of air raid wardens should advance on progressive lines in accordance with the principles explained in Air Raid Precautions Memorandum No. 9 (Notes on Training and Exercises), and following a logical sequence of subjects.

As explained in that memorandum, progressive training for air raid precautions services should be conducted in two distinct phases—INDIVIDUAL and COLLECTIVE.

This principle applies with force to air raid wardens, who must be thoroughly trained as individuals in every detail of their duties, and so trained collectively that appropriate units in any given locality know how to work as a team, and are fully competent to deal with any situation that may arise.

In addition to the full course in anti-gas, *individual* training should include instruction on the subjects mentioned in sub-paragraph (1) below. The instruction should be as practical as possible, in order to make the course interesting and to ensure that individuals have a real grasp of their work.

From this stage the classes should advance to *collective* training. For this purpose individuals should be grouped to conform, as far as possible, to their actual posts in the air raid precautions organisation. The training will generally be organised and conducted by Head Wardens, under the general direction of the Chief Warden.

The subjects recommended for collective training are given in sub-paragraph (2) below. The intention is that the training should be progressive, starting with imaginary posts arranged in the seclusion of a training centre or elsewhere and working up to exercises involving a group, and use of the actual posts selected in the local authority's scheme.

The following is a summary of the subjects for individual and collective training. It is left to the discretion of the local authority to alter the sequence to meet their individual needs, or to intersperse this training with the full course in anti-gas if this method is preferred.

Detailed guidance on the syllabus is given in Section 10 of this Memorandum.

(1) INDIVIDUAL TRAINING:—

(*a*) Local air raid precautions organisation, and important facts about the locality.

(*b*) Relations with police and public.

(*c*) Air raid wardens' Household Register and fitting and distribution of respirators to the public.

(*d*) Principles of the air raid warning system and local air raid and gas warnings.

(*e*) Message writing and reporting; use of local maps.

(*f*) Elementary methods of protection against H.E. bombs.

(*g*) Methods of dealing with incendiary bombs.

(*h*) Auxiliary Fire Service organisation.

(*j*) Damage to water, gas and electricity mains and sewers.

(*k*) Equipment of wardens' posts.

(*l*) Elementary first-aid.

(2) COLLECTIVE TRAINING:—

    (*m*) The working of a post.

    (*n*) Reporting.

    (*o*) Incidents.

    (*p*) Action after a raid.

9. Instructors for Air Raid Wardens

The individual training of wardens should be given by the following instructors:—

Subject.	*Instructor.*
Anti-gas course.	An Instructor (C.A.G.S. or A.R.P.S.*) or an Instructor (L.A.G.C. or L.A.R.P.*).
(*b*)	By arrangement with the Chief Officer of Police.
(*f*) (*g*) }	An Instructor (A.R.P.S.*) or an Instructor (L.A.R.P.*).
(*h*)	By arrangement with the Chief Officer of the Fire Brigade.
(*l*)	Under arrangements made by the Medical Officer of Health.
(*a*) (*c*) (*d*) (*e*) (*j*) (*k*)	By a suitable instructor drawn from the wardens' organisation or from the general air raid precautions organisation of the local authority (four instructors should be sufficient for a group).

Instructors drawn from the wardens' organisation should be very carefully selected from the Head, Deputy Head, Senior and Second Wardens. They should first be given a course of instruction in such of the six subjects shown above as they

---

* In view of the extended courses of training which are now being introduced at the Home Office Schools at Falfield and Easingwold, persons passing through the courses at these Schools, and the local instructors who are given the extended training, will hereafter be known as Instructors (A.R.P.S.) and (L.A.R.P.) respectively, instead of " C.A.G.S." and " L.A.G.C." as hitherto. Arrangements will be made to enable existing C.A.G.S. and L.A.G.C. Instructors to qualify for the new titles.

are to teach, and should be given practice in the art of instruction before they are considered qualified to instruct. They will be eligible for an honorarium of 5s. for each lecture given by them on the above six subjects.

10. Syllabus of Training for Air Raid Wardens

I. INDIVIDUAL TRAINING (OTHER THAN ANTI-GAS)

Index No.	Subject.	References.
W.1.	*Local air raid precautions organisation.*	(*a*) Local air raid precautions scheme. (*b*) A.R.P. Memorandum No. 4. (*c*) A.R.P. Memorandum No. 6 (a new edition will be issued shortly). (*d*) A.R.P. Handbook No. 8.

Instruction under this heading should give trainees a thorough grounding in the local air raid precautions organisation, in so far as it affects air raid wardens. It should also include a lecture on local communications and the report centre organisation.

W.2. *Important facts about the locality.*

Under this heading it should be explained to trainees what sort of details they ought to know about their immediate neighbourhood. Examples are:—

(i) Fire fighting arrangements.

(ii) Police organisation in sector, including positions of police boxes.

(iii) Electricity, water and gas authorities.

(iv) Vulnerable points (e.g., electrical installations, petrol and explosives stores, etc.).

(v) Public shelters.

(vi) Telephones for use in emergency.

(vii) Garages.

(viii) Doctors, nurses, chemists and veterinary surgeons.

(ix) Personalities.

(x) Care of the aged, infirm and blind, etc.

(xi) Situation of neighbouring wardens' posts.

(xii) Position of important turn-off cocks and switches.

W.3.	*Relations with the police and the public.*	(*a*) A.R.P Memorandum No. 4. (*b*) A.R.P. Handbook No. 8.

At this stage it should be explained to trainees how the wardens' organisation works in with the police. The broad principles are explained in the appropriate A.R.P. publications, but details differ according to the locality and trainees must be fully informed on this subject.

As regards relations with the public, here again the broad principles are explained in the appropriate A.R.P. publications, but trainees should be given detailed guidance on this point, emphasis being laid on the importance of obtaining and maintaining control over the public when incidents occur in their sector.

W.4. *Household register and the fitting and distribution of respirators.*

(a) Circular letters 702,445/3 of 6th July, and 702,445/30 of 28th October, 1938.
(b) A.R.P. Memorandum No. 4.

Trainees should be made familiar with the local forms and household register introduced for air raid wardens' use, and the method proposed for keeping these records up to date should be explained in detail.

A further lecture should be devoted to the local organisation for the storage and distribution of respirators, with guidance about local arrangements for fitting respirators and recording results.

W.5. (i) *Principles of the air raid warning system.*
(ii) *Local air raid and gas warnings.*

A.R.P. Memorandum No. 8.

(a) A.R.P. Memorandum No. 8.
(b) A.R.P. Handbook No. 8.

Trainees should have a general knowledge of the air raid warning system for the United Kingdom and know all about the local warning organisation and the signals authorised for wardens to indicate " Action Warning "—" Gas "—" All clear."

W.6. (a) *Message writing and reporting.*
(b) *Use of local maps.*

(a) A.R.P. Memorandum No. 6 (a new edition will be issued shortly).
(b) Circular letter 703,214/9 of 30th November, 1938.

(a) Once the general principles and the authorised forms have been described, this instruction becomes a matter of practice.

The amount of practice required will depend upon the previous training and experience of individuals, but the aim must be to get all trainees proficient before collective training is started (with and without respirators).

(b) Trainees should be given instruction in the local maps which have been adopted for air raid precautions use, and which they may come across in the course of their duty.

W.7.	*Elementary methods of protection against H.E. bombs.*	(a) A.R.P. Handbook No. 6. (b) " The Protection of your Home against air raids."

The aim should be to give wardens the knowledge necessary to enable them to advise and assist householders in protecting themselves and their property against H.E. bombs. Instruction should be kept simple, bearing in mind that strength of buildings and structural details are the province of appropriate technical authorities. Instruction should include:—

(a) Selection, preparation and strengthening of refuge rooms.

(b) Trench siting and digging, and construction of simple dugouts.

(c) Sandbags and other forms of protection against splinters.

(d) Action when in vicinity of unexploded bombs.

W.8.	*Methods of dealing with incendiary bombs.*	A.R.P. Handbook No. 9 (to be published shortly).

Here again, one of the objects should be to enable wardens to give advice and assistance to householders. Instructions should commence with details of the type of bomb likely to be used, its capabilities and the importance of removing inflammable materials from attics and top floors. This should be followed by a description of the technique for dealing with the bomb, and of the appliances which can be used. The instruction should conclude with demonstrations and individual practice with the stirrup pump.

W.9.	*Auxiliary Fire Service organisation.*	Memoranda and circulars issued by the Home Office (Fire Brigades Division) and the Scottish Office:— Emergency Fire Brigade Organisation, 23rd February, 1937.

W.9. *Auxiliary Fire Service*
organisation—cont.

Sketch of Emergency Fire
Brigade Organisation for
a hypothetical town.
15th December, 1937
(Scottish Office, 17th
February, 1938).

Specifications for Auxiliary
Fire Service Uniforms
and Equipment, 15th
June, 1938.

Auxiliary Fire Service
Badges, 24th August,
1938.

Memorandum on Emergency Fire Brigade
Measures in Rural Districts, 1938 (Scottish
Office, Memorandum on
Emergency Fire Brigade
Measures in Landward
Areas, 1938).

Circular letter on the Fire
Brigades Act, 27th September, 1938 (Scottish
Office, circular letter on
Fire Brigades Act, 8th
November, 1938).

Notes on various points
arising out of submission
of air raid fire precautions schemes, 24th
October, 1938, England
and Wales only. A
similar memorandum as
regards Scotland may be
obtained if required from
the Scottish Office.

Memorandum on Emergency Fire Brigade
Appliances, October,
1938.

Instruction under this head would be arranged by the Chief
Officer of the Fire Brigade and might be given in part by
officers of the Auxiliary Fire Service.

(*a*) *General organisation of the Fire Service.*

Under the Fire Brigades Act, 1938, the following are constituted Fire Authorities, (*a*) in England and Wales, all Borough

Councils, Urban District Councils and Rural District Councils
(County Councils, excepting the London County Council, have
no fire brigade responsibilities), and (b) in Scotland, all County
and Town Councils. Under the Fire Brigades Act, fire authorities are responsible for arranging schemes of mutual assistance, and, in an emergency, wider schemes for the co-ordina-
tion of fire brigades for mutual assistance, organised on a
regional basis under the directions of the Home Office, would
be brought into operation under emergency powers.

(b) General organisation of the Auxiliary Fire Service and Local Emergency Fire Brigade Measures.

All fire authorities, excepting Rural District Councils in
England and Wales, are required, under the Air Raid Precautions Act, 1937, to prepare and submit an air raid fire
precautions scheme to the Home Office or, in the case of Scotland, to the Scottish Office. The general scope of the
emergency measures has been laid down in the Memorandum
of 23rd February, 1937, supplemented by other Memoranda
(see list above). These schemes include provision for the formation of a local Auxiliary Fire Service, their training and equipment with appliances issued for their use by the Home Office or
the Scottish Office, as the case may be, and their organisation,
generally on the basis of a system of patrols, equipped with
trailer pumps, and supported by more powerful appliances at
permanent and auxiliary fire stations.

Wardens should be familiar with the local emergency fire
brigade organisation, the position of auxiliary fire stations, the
patrol routes (where patrols are organised) and all other particulars necessary to ensure efficient co-operation with the Fire
Service. It should be noted that the object of the patrol system
is to provide means by which fires may be observed and dealt
with promptly by a fire fighting unit, even if premises have
been vacated or communications have broken down.

(c) Co-operation of wardens in an emergency.

Wardens should be instructed as to the action they should
take in co-operation with the fire service, more particularly in
the event of the fall of bombs. The following matters, in
particular, should be dealt with:—

(i) Action on the fall of an incendiary bomb (depending
on whether there is or is not danger of a fire resulting).

(ii) Action if a fire is observed or reported (depending
on whether a patrol system has or has not been organised).
Generally speaking, if there is an effective system of patrols,
the wardens should first endeavour to call a patrol unit.

(iii) Action if a road on a fire patrol route is blocked by
debris or gas, in particular the steps to warn the patrols

against entering the blocked road, unless actually required for fire extinction.

(iv) Arrangements for employment of fire patrols as part of the available means of communication with auxiliary fire stations, report centres, etc.

(v) Means which should be used by wardens to attract the attention of fire patrols by day and by night in the absence of street and other lights.

W.10. *Damage to water,*
    gas and electric
    mains and sewers.

Trainees should be instructed how to recognise damage, assess its importance and danger and know how to act pending the arrival of trained personnel.

W.11. *Equipment of war-*   A.R.P. Memorandum No. 4.
    den's post.

The nature of the equipment and how to store, maintain and use the various articles.

W.12. *Elementary first aid.*   Circular letter No. 16/1939
                                   of 26th January, 1939.

A short course of first aid instruction of a general character.

II. COLLECTIVE TRAINING.

W.T.1. *The working of a*
    post.

Training should start with a single post, and work up to a group of posts, exercises being carried out in such routine work as:—

(*a*) Duties in peace.

(*b*) Distribution of respirators.

(*c*) Manning a post.

(*d*) Assumption of duties.

(*e*) Patrols.

(*f*) Action on hearing " Air Raid Warning."

W.T.2. *Reporting.*

Use of authorised message pads. Practice by day and night in message writing and telephoning. Inter-communication when an incident occurs at a distance from the wardens' post. Alternative methods of reporting if normal channels fail.

W.T.3. *Incidents.*

Commencing with a single post and working up to two or more as local conditions require, training should be given in such matters as:—

    (*a*) Action if the presence of gas is suspected or known.

    (*b*) Action on the fall of:—
        (i) H.E. bombs.
        (ii) Incendiary bombs.

    (*c*) Action in case of panic.

    (*d*) Dealing with casualties.

    (*e*) Guidance of Rescue, First Aid, Auxiliary Fire and other parties.

    (*f*) Maintaining touch with adjacent posts, and reinforcement of adjoining sectors.

W.T.4. *Action after a raid.*

Wardens will need to be carefully instructed and exercised in their responsibilities and duties at the two stages immediately following a raid and identified by the appropriate signals for " Raiders Passed " and " All Clear." Trainees might be exercised in such matters as:—

    (*a*) Reconnaissance of sector to ascertain any further action required on incidents already reported.

    (*b*) Reports of incidents which have hitherto escaped notice.

    (*c*) Control of residents and general public.

    (*d*) Reporting " All Clear " when satisfied that sector is safe from gas.

    (*e*) Removal and temporary accommodation of persons rendered homeless.

INSPECTION AND REPAIR OF RESPIRATORS AND OILSKIN CLOTHING

CONTENTS

INSPECTION AND REPAIR OF RESPIRATORS AND OILSKIN CLOTHING

INTRODUCTION

This Memorandum contains notes on the inspection of respirators and oilskin clothing, together with instructions with regard to local repairs where these are possible. Particulars regarding children's respirators and babies' anti-gas helmets are added in this edition, together with the instructions for the repair of oilskin garments, previously published in another form.

The section on the Care of Respirators which was contained in the 1st edition has been omitted because the information is being transferred to a new edition of A.R.P. Handbook No. 1.

Scheme-making local authorities have already been asked to arrange for the establishment of one or more **Repair Depots** for respirators and oilskin clothing, under the charge, for preference, of Instructors holding Special or First Class Certificates, A.R.P.S. or C.A.G.S. The number of these Depots must be kept at a minimum to economise both the employment of staff and the provision of the special tools and equipment required.

Each Repair Depot should be provided with a suitable room, with a bench and the necessary tools, and should have, besides the Instructor in charge, a definite staff earmarked and trained to work in it as required. Supplies of certain spare parts and special tools for the repair of respirators, and materials for the repair of oilskin garments, will be issued by the Ministry of Home Security to authorities who set up Repair Depots in accordance with the Ministry's instructions, the issue being regulated in accordance with the numbers of respirators or garments to be serviced from each depot.

1. Inspection of Respirators and Oilskin Clothing

Inspection of respirators should be a matter of regular routine.

It should be the business of the wardens in each sector to visit the inhabitants of the sector once a month and inspect their respirators. At this inspection, the opportunity should be taken (where this is not known to have been done already) to ensure that the respirator has been properly fitted to the individual, and the straps of the harness pinned in the proper position. Where Contex is fitted, it should be examined to ensure that the correct method of affixing has been carried out, and the condition of the adhesive tape is satisfactory. Advice should also be given about the form of carrier and its protection against wet. The dangers of unsuitable carriers, if found, should be pointed out, and it should be emphasized that the local authority cannot guarantee replacement of respirators damaged from such a cause.

As regards Service and Civilian Duty respirators, the individual who would wear them should be made to inspect them frequently—i.e. after every occasion on which the respirator is worn, and at least once a week if it is not worn—and to draw attention to any defects. In addition, the officer in charge of the depot or the head warden should make it a practice to have a complete inspection of all the respirators in his charge once a month. Whenever it can be managed, the officer in charge* of the Repair Depot should attend at this inspection, and his advice should always be sought whenever a defective respirator is found or suspected. It should in any case be arranged that he inspects all the Service and C.D. respirators within the area for which he is responsible at least once every three months.

Similar arrangements should be made for the regular inspection of oilskin clothing held by services.

Respirators and oilskin clothing in store should be inspected by the officer in charge of the Repair Depot at least once every three months. In the case of respirators, it will usually be necessary only to inspect about 10 % of stocks, provided that storage conditions are good and that the 10 % is selected to be truly representative of the whole stock. If defects are found in the 10 % inspected, a further 10 % should be examined, and if this second lot is unsatisfactory, inspection of the whole stock should be undertaken. In the case of oilskin clothing, 100 % should be inspected if possible, because of the benefit of turning over oilskin fabric garments from time to time. Any garments which have become tacky should be removed.

The officer in charge of the Repair Depot should take charge of all Service and Civilian Duty respirators and oilskin garments found to be defective, and should deal with them in accordance with the instructions in the following sections.

2. Repair of Respirators

The officer in charge of the Repair Depot will be responsible for examining all Service and C.D. respirators passed to him as unserviceable or suspected unserviceable, and for classifying them as follows:—

1. " S."	. . . . . .	Serviceable
or 2. " R."	. . . . .	Repairable locally
or 3. " B.L.R."	. . . . .	Beyond Local Repair

Those classified " B.L.R." must be returned to the Regional Store for the particular region, accompanied by the particulars indicated in Appendix A.

The classification " R."—repairable locally—will be used only for defects coming within the following classes of repairs. These are the only repairs which may be carried out locally, and normally they will be executed at the Repair Depot. Instructions for carrying out these repairs are contained in Appendix B, which is divided into Parts and headings as follows:—

Part 1—General Civilian Respirators.

G.C. 1. Changing container.
G.C. 2. Changing rubber band.
G.C. 3. Changing inlet valve on container.
G.C. 4. Changing contex on container.
G.C. 5. Repair of torn or punctured facepieces.
G.C. 6. Replacement of safety pins.

Part 2—Small Children's Respirators.

S.C. 1. Repair of head harness.
S.C. 2. Changing container.
S.C. 3. Changing inlet valve on container.
S.C. 4. Changing contex on container.
S.C. 5. Repair of torn or punctured facepieces.

---

* The term " officer in charge " in this Memorandum includes, for purposes of a large Repair Depot, any assistant who is an Instructor, A.R.P.S. or C.A.G.S.

Part 3—Babies' Anti-Gas Helmets.

B.H. 1. Changing container or inlet valve on bellows.
B.H. 2. Changing contex on container.
B.H. 3. Repair of damaged bags and air supply units.
B H. 4. Repair of bent frames.

Part 4—Civilian Duty Respirators.

C.D. 1. Replacement of head harness.
C.D. 2. Replacement of toggle clip.
C.D. 3. Changing container.
C.D. 4. Changing inlet valve on container.
C.D. 5. Changing contex on container.
C.D. 6. Changing eyepiece discs.
C.D. 7. Repairs to haversacks.

Part 5—Service Respirators.

S. 1. Replacement of head harness.
S. 2. Re-wiring connecting tube at either end.
S. 3. Changing container.
S. 4. Changing inlet valve.
S. 5. Changing outlet valve.
S. 6. Changing eyepiece discs.
S. 7. Repairs to stockinette.
S. 8. Repairs to haversacks.

3. Repair of Oilskin Clothing

The arrangements for classifying garments as " S.," " R." and " B.L.R." should be the same as described in the preceding section for respirators.

Those classified " B.L.R." should be reported to the Director of Supply, for instructions as to disposal. *They should not automatically be sent to the Regional Store.* When the instructions are received, the articles should be despatched with the particulars indicated in Appendix A.

The classification " R."—repairable locally—should be used for the defects described in Appendix C, which contains instructions for their repair. There is no provision for local repairs of heavy oilskins, which must all be classified " B.L.R." when no longer serviceable. The classification " R." is applicable to garments made of fabric D, in respect of the following types of repair only:—

Light oilskin jackets and trousers.

Hoods.

Curtains.

1. Patching tears.
2. Replacing damaged or missing press fasteners.
3. Doping *small* areas of rubbed or cracked surfaces.

Gloves.

Doping *small* abrasions or cracks.

APPENDIX A

PROCEDURE FOR RETURN OF RESPIRATORS AND OILSKIN GARMENTS " B.L.R."

Each batch of respirators or oilskin garments returned to the Ministry's Store as being " Beyond Local Repair " should be accompanied by a schedule in one of the forms given below.

Except in the case of General Civilian respirators, each respirator or garment should have a tie-on label attached to it bearing the name of the local authority or police authority, the date (as on the schedule), a note of the defect, and a number corresponding with the item number in the schedule. (These numbers should run from one upwards in each schedule.)

In the case of General Civilian respirators, components having the same type of defect may be tied together and labelled in bulk, the number of items in each bundle being marked on the label as well as the particulars enumerated above.

The schedules should be on the following lines:—

SCHEDULE OF RESPIRATORS

RETURNED BY [Local Authority or Police Authority] FROM   REPAIR DEPOT

1. Item No. of respirator	2. Type of respirator	3. Size	4. Nature of defect
No. 1	S. Mk. IV (or V)	Large	Eyepiece inner rims damaged.
No. 2	C.D.	Normal	Facepiece torn.
No. 3	Baby's helmet bag.	—	Badly torn.
No. 4	G.C. facepieces (47 in all)	10 Large 37 Medium	Damaged eye panels.
No. 5	G.C. facepieces (62 in all)	5 Large 40 Medium 17 Small	Rubber badly torn.
Etc.	Etc.	Etc.	Etc.

SCHEDULE OF OILSKIN GARMENTS

RETURNED BY [Local Authority or Police Authority] FROM   REPAIR DEPOT

1. Item No. of Garment	2. Nature of Garment (including size if appropriate)	3. Nature of Defect
No. 1	Light jacket	Badly torn
No. 2	1 pr. gloves, large	Oiled surface badly abraded
Etc.	Etc.	Etc.

Instructions for Repair of Respirators

PART 1.—GENERAL CIVILIAN RESPIRATORS

Materials and Tools Required

I. *Materials*

Store	Required for	Stores Nomenclature
Adhesive tape	Affixing Contex	Tape, Adhesive 1"
Pins, Safety	Harness, G.C. type	Pins, Safety
Rubber band	Affixing Container, G.C. type	Rubber Band
Rubber Patches	Repairing Facepieces, G.C. type	(For local purchase)
Rubber Solution	Ditto	Ditto
Valve, Inlet (black rubber)	Container, G.C. type	Valve, Inlet No. 1

II. *Tools*

None

G.C. 1. Changing Container (G.C. type).

Materials.—Rubber band.

The defective container is removed and the new container fitted as laid down in A.R.P. Handbook No. 1 (2nd Ed.) Appendix D, para. 4 (ii) and (iii), a new rubber band being fitted if the old one shows any sign of deterioration.

G.C. 2. Changing Rubber Band (G.C. type).

See G.C. 1 above.

G.C. 3. Changing Inlet Valve on Container (G.C. type).

Lift the old valve off the stud, and fit the new valve by stretching the hole in the centre over the head of the stud. It is important that the valve should be pressed down to the base of the stud.

G.C. 4. Changing Contex on Container (G.C. type).

Materials.—24" of 1" adhesive tape.

(i) Place the Contex, *with its smooth recessed face and rim uppermost*, on a table about one inch from the edge. If the table is polished or very smooth it is advisable to interpose a pad of newspaper to prevent the Contex from slipping and scratching the polished surface.

(ii) Stand the respirator container symmetrically on top of the Contex so that the rims of the container and Contex are together. Place the headharness inside the facepiece out of the way.

(iii) Measure and cut off a 24" length of the 1" wide adhesive tape supplied.

(iv) Hold the respirator container and Contex firmly together on the table, and lay one end of the length of tape lengthwise over the two protruding rims so that the tape lies equally on the container and on the Contex (see fig. 1). Press the end of the tape firmly in contact so that it adheres, and then slowly rotate the respirator and Contex so that the tape is wound symmetrically over the join an inch or so at a time. *Pull the tape tightly while it is being wound on.* When the tape has been wound once around the joint, lift the respirator from the table and with the fingers smooth the tape already wound on so that it becomes moulded closely to the shape of the protruding rims and its edges lie flat on the container and Contex. Then hold the respirator with the Contex resting in the palm of the hand and the facepiece away from the body, and continue to wind tightly the remainder of the tape so that it covers the first turn evenly and neatly (see fig. 2). Finally, smooth the tape as before and make sure in particular that the end is firmly stuck down.

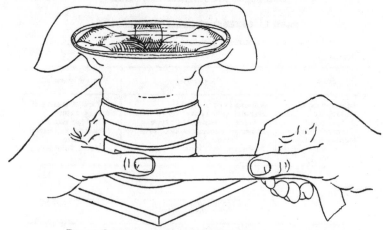

FIG. 1.—STARTING TO WIND ADHESIVE TAPE FOR AFFIXING CONTEX.

(v) If any puckers or irregularities are formed during winding they should either be smoothed out and pressed flat, or the tape unwound slightly so as to remove them. The 24″ length of tape allows two turns around the joint with a small overlap at the end.

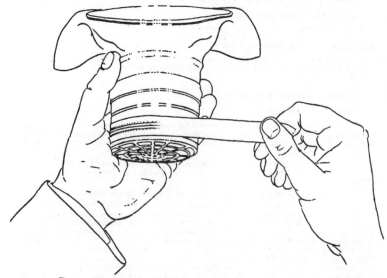

FIG. 2.—WINDING THE SECOND TURN OF ADHESIVE TAPE ON CONTEX.

G.C. 5. Repair of Torn or Punctured Facepieces (G.C. type).

Materials.—Rubber patches, solution, etc.

Facepieces of General Civilian respirators which have a small tear, slit or perforation in the rubber portion can be repaired by patching in the same way as a cycle tyre. No repair should be attempted of a tear which extends to the edge of the facepiece, or of a puncture or tear which comes within ¼ inch of the eye panel.

The facepiece should first be removed from the container, and the patch should be put on the outside. Vulcanising is *not* to be adopted.

In the case of a slit the patch should not be less than ¼ inch longer than the slit at each end. In general the smallest size patch which will give a safe repair should be used. For simple punctures which are visible only when the rubber is stretched a circular patch ½ inch in diameter is adequate.

Prepared patches as sold for the repair of cycle tyres should be used, and the maker's instructions as to the method of using them should be followed. Repair outfits for the purpose should be purchased locally.

If prepared patches are not available, a piece of rubber cut from a badly torn facepiece may be used, but in that case the surface of the patch will need to be carefully prepared before the solution is applied, in the manner required for patching cycle tyres. A facepiece with a broken eye panel, but otherwise serviceable, should not be mutilated, but should be kept for return to the Regional Store.

G.C. 6. Replacement of Safety Pins (G.C. type).

Safety pins on the harness of General Civilian facepieces which have become lost or excessively rusty should be replaced.

If the facepiece is on issue to an individual care must be taken that the position of the pins is not altered.

PART 2.—SMALL CHILDREN'S RESPIRATORS

MATERIALS AND TOOLS REQUIRED

I. *Materials.*

Store	Required for	Stores Nomenclature
Adhesive tape	Affixing Contex	Tape, Adhesive 1″
Rubber patches	Repairing facepieces, S.C. type	(For local purchase)
Rubber solution	Ditto	Ditto
Valve, Inlet (red rubber)	Container, S.C. type	Valve, Inlet No. 1 (S.C. type)

II. *Tools.*

None

S.C. 1. Repair of Head Harness (S.C. type).

If, through rough use, the end of the blue braid sleeving has been pulled out of either of the metal end clips which secure the springs to the facepiece, the harness should be examined to see if it is fit for repair.

Slip the braid back from the metal clip and examine the spring for about an inch of its length near the clip. If the spring is intact, i.e. if it has not been over-stretched so that the coils are opened widely, and if its length, measured to the central clip, is no more than ¼ inch longer than that of the other half of the same spring attached to the opposite side of the facepiece, the harness is fit to repair.

The repair is to be carried out in the following manner:—Ease the end of the braid forward over the outside of the barrel of the clip until it is pressed against the edge of the rubber. Cut off a 12-inch length of sewing thread (black or blue) and bind it very tightly and evenly over the braid on the barrel of the clip. Finish off by knotting the ends securely. Then trim off the loose ends of thread and any ragged ends of braid which project from under the binding.

S.C. 2. Changing Container (S.C. type).

The defective container is removed by unscrewing it from the metal holder, which is permanently fixed in the facepiece. The new container is screwed fully home into the holder so that it is a tight hand fit. On no account must the bound joint around the metal holder be interfered with.

S.C 3. Changing Inlet Valve on Container (S.C. type).

The procedure is the same as for the General Civilian type—see G.C. 3 in Part 1.

S.C. 4. Changing Contex on Container (S.C. type).

Materials.—24″ of 1″ adhesive tape.

The procedure is the same as for the General Civilian type—see G.C. 4 in Part 1.

S.C. 5. Repair of Torn or Punctured Facepieces (S.C. type).

Materials.—Rubber patches, solution, etc.

Small tears, slits or perforations in the facepiece of Small Children's respirators can be patched in the same way as General Civilian facepieces—see G.C. 5 in Part 1.

PART 3.—BABIES' ANTI-GAS HELMETS

MATERIALS AND TOOLS REQUIRED

I. *Materials.*

Store	Required for	Stores Nomenclature
Adhesive tape	Affixing Contex	Tape, Adhesive 1″
Ditto	Binding rubber elbow and bellows on container, B.H. type	Tape, Adhesive ¾″
Rubber patches	Repairing bag, B.H. type	(For local purchase)
Rubber solution	Ditto	Ditto
Screws	Adjusting tailpiece on frame, B.H. type	Screws, Tail-piece (B.H.)
Tape	Replacing draw-tape on bag, B.H. type	(For local purchase)
Valve, Inlet (black rubber)	Container, C.D. type	Valve, Inlet No. 1

II. *Tools.*

None

B.H. 1. Changing Container or Inlet Valve on Bellows (B.H. type).

Materials.—15″ of ¾″ adhesive tape (if required).

Note.—A C.D. type container is supplied with a Baby's Helmet, but a G.C. type container may be used if a C.D. type is not available.

(i) Release the fabric strap which holds the air supply unit to the metal frame. Do not release the metal clip which fastens the rubber elbow to the bag.

(ii) Carefully remove the adhesive tape which is wound round the middle of the unit. In the majority of cases the tape can be used again, and with this object in view it should not be allowed either to turn back on itself or stick to any surface or become dirty.

(iii) Slip the bellows off the container, and remove the container and the rubber mounting carrying the two valves, from the rubber elbow piece. Slip the valve mounting off the container and replace it fully home on the new container, taking note that it should be fitted on the valve end of the container and that no valve is to be fitted on the stud on the container. Replace the container in the rubber elbow so that the two valves are positioned with their edges towards the inlet into the helmet. Inspect the inlet valve on the inside of the bellows and if it is defective, replace it by a new one. Then replace the bellows on the container so that the arrow head moulded on the flat portion of the open end of the bellows is pointing towards the similar arrow on the rubber elbow piece, and the protruding rim on the end of the container is positioned in the moulded groove 1¼ inches from the open end of the bellows. There will then be a gap of about one-eighth of an inch between the elbow and the bellows.

(iii) Replace the adhesive tape (which was removed under (ii) above) round the middle of the unit. It should be bound tightly and symmetrically over the adjacent ends of the bellows and elbow so that the gap is covered. If the tape has lost some of its stickiness this can sometimes be refreshed by warming the sticky side *very* slightly. It is advantageous to place the end of the tape, which was outside to begin with, on the inside when replacing it. If the tape is completely unsuitable a new 15″ length of ¾″ wide tape should be cut and used.

(iv) Re-attach the air supply unit to the frame by means of the strap.

B.H. 2. Changing Contex on Container (B.H. type).

Materials.—24″ of 1″ adhesive tape; 15″ of ¾″ adhesive tape (if required).

(i) Disconnect the air supply unit from the bag by loosening the screw clip. Then release the fabric strap and detach the complete air supply unit from the helmet.

(ii) Carefully remove the adhesive tape which is wound round the middle of the unit and slip the bellows off the container. In the majority of instances the tape can be used again and with this end in view do not allow it to turn back on itself or stick to any surface or become dirty. Do not remove the elbow on the opposite end of the container.

(iii) Attach a Contex to the exposed end of the container in the manner described under G.C. 4 in Part 1.

(iv) Replace the bellows on the container so that the arrow head moulded on the flat portion of the open end of the bellows is pointing towards the similar arrow on the rubber elbow piece, and the protruding rim in the centre of the joint between the container and Contex is positioned in the moulded groove 1¼ inches from the open end of the bellows. There will then be a gap of about one-eighth of an inch between the elbow and bellows.

(v) Replace the adhesive tape (which was removed under (ii) above) round the middle of the unit in the manner described in B.H. 1 (iii) above.

(vi) Replace the air supply unit on the helmet, making sure that the screw clip and the strap are tight.

B.H. 3. Repair of Damaged Bags and Air Supply Units (B.H. type).

Materials.—Rubber patches, solution, etc.; thread; tape.

Tears, punctures or slits in the bag portion of helmets, or in any of the rubber components of the air supply units (except the valves which are not repairable), may be repaired by means of patches as described under G.C. 5 in Part 1. The patches should be put on the outside rubber surface of the bag portion.
Tapes which have become detached from the bag portion should be re-stitched securely in position. Missing tapes should be replaced by any suitable tape available locally.

B.H. 4. Repair of Bent Frames (B.H. type).

Materials.—Screws, tail-piece (B.H.) (if required).

Metal frames which have become distorted or bent should be straightened so as to restore them as near as possible to their original shape. Where necessary the frames should be re-touched with paint of similar shade to the original coating.
Missing screws for adjusting the tail-piece on the frame should be replaced.

PART 4.—CIVILIAN DUTY RESPIRATORS

MATERIALS AND TOOLS REQUIRED

I. *Materials.*

Store	Required for	Stores Nomenclature
Adhesive Tape	Affixing Contex	Tape, Adhesive 1″
Elastic Webbing	Head Harness, C.D. type	Elastic Webbing, ¾″ wide
Eyepiece Discs	Eyepiece, C.D. type	Discs, Eyepiece 2½″ C.D. Mk. I
Eyepiece Washers	Eyepiece, C.D. type	Washer, Eyepiece
Harness Pads	Head Harness, C.D. type	Pads, Harness
Loops	Head Harness, C.D. type	Loops Mk. I C.D.
Mineral Jelly	Eyepiece Discs	(For local purchase)
Tags	Head Harness, C.D. type	Tags, Mk. I C.D.
Thread	Haversack, C.D. type	(For local purchase)
Toggle Clips	Attaching Container, C.D. type	Toggle Clip (C.D.)
Valve, Inlet (black rubber)	Container, C.D. type	Valve Inlet No. 1
Whipcord	Haversack, C.D. type	Whipcord

II. *Tools.*

Tool	Required for
Eyepiece Removal Tool	Changing eyepiece discs
Hammer 8 oz. (1″ face) (local purchase)	Head harness repair
Needles (local purchase)	Haversack repair
Pliers, side-cutting, 6″ or 8″ (local purchase)	Head harness repair
Scissors (local purchase)	Head harness and haversack repair

C.D. 1. Replacement of Head Harness (C.D. type).

Materials.—Canvas backed rubber-pad; elastic webbing; tags; loops.

Tools.—Scissors, hammer with 1″ face, pliers.

Civilian Duty respirators may be supplied with Harness Mk. I (C.D. type) or Harness No. 4 Mk. III.

The elastic bands of the former type cannot be replaced individually, and to effect repair the whole harness must be replaced by Harness No. 4, Mk. III. This harness consists of three lengths of elastic webbing each 18 inches long threaded through slots in a rubber pad.

The defective harness or elastic band is to be removed by cutting off the tags, and pulling the elastic bands out of the buckles of the mask. The new elastics are assembled and fitted as shown in fig. 3.

The elastic webbing is supplied in rolls from which 18-inch lengths should be cut with clean square ends.

Threading elastics

Top bands.—Hold the head pad with the rough side uppermost, thread the length of elastic downwards through slot A, and draw through until 8 inches remain unthreaded. Continue threading the same end successively upwards and downwards through slots B, C and D. The two ends for attachment to the facepiece should then be of an equal length within ¼ inch.

Right side and left bottom bands.—Thread the length of elastic *upwards* through slot *e* until 8 inches remain unthreaded. Thread successively down and up through slots *f*, *g* and *h*.

Left side and right bottom bands.—Thread the length of elastic through slots E, F, G and H in turn.

NOTE.—It is important to avoid stretching the elastic between the slots.

Attachment of harness to facepiece

The head harness should be attached to the facepiece so that the smooth side of the rubber pad is next to the head when the facepiece is worn. The ends of elastic are threaded through the facepiece buckles and secured by means of tags and loops as follows:—

The six ends of the elastic webbing are threaded first through loops and then through the appropriate buckles on the mask, the ends attached to the acute angle of the pad passing to the two buckles at the top of the mask respectively. The elastic bands pass through the buckle from the inside of the facepiece to the outside, and are then passed over the sliding piece of the buckles and back through the buckle again at the crimped end

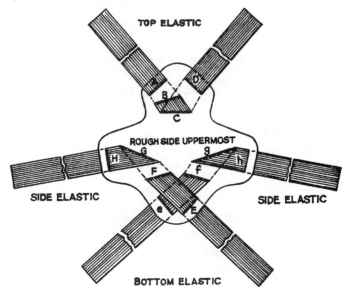

FIG. 3.—THREADING ELASTICS FOR HEAD HARNESS.

Each end is then brought back to the loop, through which is placed a tag, the tag being held, open edge outwards, and the end of the webbing placed in it after having been doubled over to the extent of ¼ inch, and secured by closing the tag on to it by a few taps with a hammer, or with pliers, so as to grip the webbing firmly. Care should be taken to see that the tag is closed along its entire length. In the final position there must be no twists in the elastics, and the split ends of the loops must in every case be inside the tags.

C.D. 2. Replacement of Toggle Clip (C.D. type).

Containers of C.D. respirators may be fitted with binding wire and rubber tape or with a toggle clip. When replacement is undertaken it should be by toggle clip in either case. See that the container is fitting properly against the flange on the inside of the facepiece and that the clip is lying snugly in the channel on the outside of the facepiece before tightening up. The hook and fastener of the toggle clip should be located adjacent to the chin of the mask.

C.D. 3. Changing Container (C.D. type).

Materials.—Toggle clip (if required).

The defective container is removed by cutting the binding wire or undoing the toggle clip. The new container is inserted in the facepiece up to the flange at the back of the orifice and is then secured by a toggle clip, which should be fitted as in C.D. 2 above.

C.D. 4. Changing Inlet Valve on Container (C.D. type).

The procedure is the same as for the G.C. container—see G.C. 3 in Part 1.

C.D. 5. Changing Contex on Container (C.D. type).

Materials.—24" of 1" adhesive tape.

The procedure is the same as for the G.C. container—see G.C. 4 in Part 1.

C.D. 6. Changing Eyepiece Discs (C.D. type).

Materials.—Plain glass discs (C.D. type); eyepiece washers; mineral jelly.

Tool.—Eyepiece removal tool.

Grasp the eyepiece on the inside of the facepiece with one hand. With the other hand engage the eyepiece removal tool in the slots cut in the eyepiece rim and unscrew in an anti-clockwise direction. Remove the defective disc and examine the rubber washer underneath the disc. If this is unduly hardened or perished replace with a new washer and insert the new disc on top of the washer. Smear the threads on the rim with a very thin coating of mineral jelly, taking care that there is no excess of grease which may come in contact with the rubber washer.

Engage the inner rim in the outer rim, taking care that the threads are not crossed: insert the eyepiece tool and screw down with a clockwise motion until friction between the rim and the glass is felt: then tighten up by giving another eighth of a turn, i.e. an amount equal to half the distance between adjacent slots.

C.D. 7. Repairs to Haversacks (C.D. type).

Materials.—Whipcord; thread.

Tools.—Needles; scissors.

Haversacks should be repaired locally as necessary so long as they are capable of repair.

PART 5.—SERVICE RESPIRATORS

MATERIALS AND TOOLS REQUIRED

I. *Materials.*

Store	Required for	Stores Nomenclature
Adhesive Tape	Connecting Tube, S. type	Tape Adhesive ½" (white)
Binding Wire	Connecting Tube, S. type	Wires Binding, 11"
Check plate	Outlet Valve, S. type, No. 2 Mk.II	Check plate Mk. I
" D " Loop 9/16"	Haversack, S. type	Loops—" D "—9/16"
" D " Loop 1"	Haversack, S. type	Loops—" D "—1"
Elastic Webbing	Head Harness, S. type	Elastic Webbing ¾" wide
Eyepiece Discs	Eyepiece, S. type	Discs, Eyepiece 2½" Mk. II
Eyepiece Washers	Eyepiece, S. type	Washer, Eyepiece
Harness Pads	Harness, S. type	Pads, Harness
Loops	Harness, S. type	Loops Mk. II (S.)
Mineral jelly	Eyepiece Discs, S. type	(For local purchase)
Rubber Solution	Stockinette, S. type	(For local purchase)
" S " Hooks	Haversack, S. type	Haversack Mk. V or VI—"S" Hook
Spring Hooks	Haversack, S. type	Haversack Mk. V or VI— Spring Hook
Slides, Shoulder Straps	Haversack, S. type	Haversack Mk. V or VI—Slide
Tags	Harness, S. type	Tags Mk. II (S.)
Thread	Haversack, S. type	(For local purchase)
Valve Inlet	Container, S. (Type E)	Valve Inlet No. 3A or No. 4
Valve Outlet	Facepiece, S. type	Valve Outlet No. 2, Mk. I or Mk. II
Whipcord	Haversack, S. type	Whipcord

II. *Tools.*

Tool	Required for
Container Detaching Tool	Container removal
Eyepiece Removal Tool	Changing eyepiece discs
Hammer 8 oz. (1" face) (local purchase)	Head harness repair
Needles (local purchase)	Haversack repair
Pliers, side-cutting, 6" or 8" (local purchase)	Head harness repair: wiring connecting tubes
Scissors (local purchase)	Head harness and haversack repair
Valve Guard Securing Key Mk.I	Outlet Valve renewal
Valve Extractor Mk. I	For Valve Inlet No. 3 or 3A
Valve Extractor Mk. II	For Valve Inlet No. 4
Valve Positioning Tool Mk. I	For Valve Inlet No. 3 or 3A
Valve Positioning Tool Mk. III	For Valve Inlet No. 4

8. 1. Replacement of Head Harness (S. type).

Materials.—Canvas-backed rubber pad; elastic webbing; tags; loops.

Tools.—Scissors, hammer with 1" face, pliers.

Service respirators may be supplied with Harness No. 4 Mk. II or Mk. III. The elastic bands of the Mk. II type can be replaced individually, and to effect repair the whole harness must be replaced by the Mk. III type. The harness consists (as in the case of the C.D. respirator) of three lengths of elastic webbing each 18 inches long threaded through slots in a rubber pad.

The procedure is exactly the same as for replacing the harness of a C.D. respirator— see under C.D. 1 in Part 4.

8. 2. Re-wiring Connecting Tube at either end (S. type).

Materials.—½" adhesive tape; 11-inch binding wires.

Tools.—Scissors, side-cutting pliers (6" or 8"), container detaching tool.

(a) Re-wiring of connecting tubes may be necessary either for the purpose of attaching a new container or after disinfection or decontamination, or to replace a rusty binding wire. If in the last case the rubber shows any signs of deterioration, the tubes will NOT be re-wired, but the tube and facepiece will be sentenced " B.L.R."

(b) In removing the old wire care must be taken to avoid damaging the connecting tube. Remove the adhesive tape protection on the twisted ends of the wire and turn up the twisted ends at right angles to the tube. Press one point of the container detaching tool under a single strand of the wire near the twisted end. On pressing over the tool, the wire will be cut by the sharp edge inside the " V." Remove the wire.

(c) The tube will be rewired in the following manner; A piece of ½" adhesive tape approximately 5 inches long is wound round the tube (overlap at the back) in the position to be occupied by the binding wire. A piece of adhesive tape 1 inch long is placed centrally on a piece of binding wire (tinned iron wire 18 S.W.G.) 11 inches long, and the wire is then passed twice round the rubber tube just above the ridge on the valve holder or below the ridge on the container neck (i.e. between the ridge and the end of the rubber tube). The ends of the wire are then twisted together with the fingers and the twist gripped with pliers. The wire is then tightened by means of a steady pull on the pliers. Without relaxing the pull, twist the wires until the slack is almost but not quite taken up. Apply a steady pull for the second time and twist the wire to take up all the slack. The turns of the wire should be firmly embedded in the adhesive tape. The twisted end should now be cut off to about ¼ inch long and turned down at right angles so as to lie flat along the tube and pointing downwards towards the container or upwards towards the facepiece. The small piece of adhesive tape is then pressed down over the ends of the wire. Wiring should be carried out with the maximum tension that can be obtained with a direct pull without over-straining. Attempts to tighten up by twisting the wire instead of by direct pull invariably cause over-strain at the point where the twist begins, and will frequently result in a broken wire, even although the actual tension on the wire is quite low

8. 3. Changing Container (S. type).

Materials.—½" adhesive tape: 11-inch binding wire.

Tools.—Scissors, detaching tool, side-cutting pliers.

The defective container is removed by unwiring as described in 2 (b) above. If the new container is of Type A or D, *first remove the cotton waste plug from the neck.* If the new container is Type E there is no cotton plug in the neck, and *care must be taken that the inlet valve which is in the neck is not interfered with or damaged in any way.*

Moisten the neck of the container and slip the corrugated rubber tube on it so that the tube reaches over the flange in the neck and down to the body of the container. Care must be taken that the facepiece is in the correct position relative to the container. When the Type E container is fitted, the air inlets should be to the wearer's left when the facepiece is adjusted, i.e. towards the centre partition of the haversack. The tube will then be wired into place as described in S. 2 above.

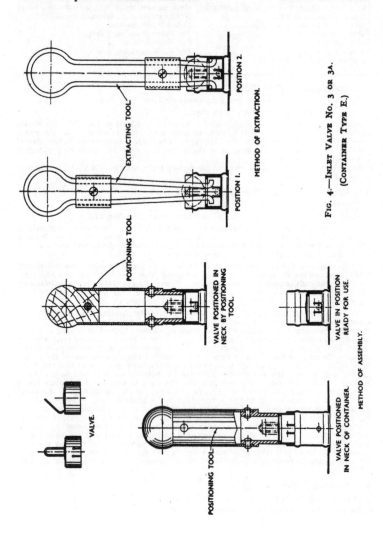

FIG. 4.—INLET VALVE No. 3 OR 3A.
(CONTAINER TYPE E.)

8. 4. Changing Inlet Valve (S. type).

Materials.—Inlet Valve No. 3A, Mk. I, or No. 4, Mk. I (container Type E).

Tools.—Valve Extracting Tool Mk. I, Valve Positioning Tool Mk. I, for Valve Inlet No. 3 or 3A: Valve Extracting Tool Mk. II, Valve Positioning Tool Mk. III, for Valve Inlet No. 4.

Containers Type E when received may be found to be fitted with Inlet Valve No. 3 or 3A (metal) or Inlet Valve No. 4 (rubber). Replacements are to be made with Inlet Valve No. 3A or Inlet Valve No. 4.

Removal of Inlet Valve No. 3 or 3A (see fig. 4).

    (i) Set the slide of the tool at the curved end and the valve flap open.

    (ii) Insert the tool in the valve till its hooked ends are under the valve seat and push the slide down so that the hooked ends are expanded and wedged under the valve seat.

    (iii) Withdraw the valve by exerting a steady pull on the tool.

Removal of Inlet Valve No. 4 (see fig. 5).

    Place the hook of the extracting tool under the bottom of the valve body (fig. 5(4)), and pull upwards with an outward pressure to prevent the hook slipping off the body.

Insertion of Inlet Valve No. 3A (see fig. 4).

    (i) Insert the valve just inside the container neck with its spring tongue pointing downwards in line with the indentation in the neck.

    (ii) Place the positioning tool on top of the valve so that the slot in the tool is clear of the wire guard on the valve, and press down until the flange of the tool rests on the top of the container neck all round.
The top of the valve will now be approximately 9/16″ below the top of the container neck.

    (iii) See that the wire guard is set at about 45° and that the valve has not been damaged during assembly and functions freely.

Insertion of Inlet Valve No. 4 (see fig. 5).

    (i) Lightly lubricate the lower end of the valve body with French chalk or water.

    (ii) Insert the valve with its flap uppermost in the neck of the container. Press down carefully until the upper edge of the valve body is just below the top of the neck. Place the positioning tool on top of the valve as shown in fig. 5(2).

    (iii) Gently press down the positioning tool until its shoulder rests on the top edge of the container neck. The valve should then be in the position shown in fig. 5(3).

    (iv) Remove the positioning tool and verify that the flap is free to move and is correctly positioned. It is essential that the valve flap should lie flat and centrally over the valve seating.
The valve should be finally examined immediately before fitting the container in the connecting tube.

8. 5. Changing Outlet Valve (S. type).

Materials.—Valve outlet No. 2 Mk. I or Mk. II; check plate Mk. I (if required).

Tool.—Valve guard securing key.

To remove the defective valve insert the pins of the key in the holes in the captive nut on the valve guard and unscrew in an anti-clockwise direction. When the nut is free from the pin, gently prize off the valve guard by inserting a pointed piece of wood or similar article in one of the holes in the guard. Remove the check plate (if fitted) and the defective valve, examine the seatings on the valve holder and see that they are clean and undamaged. If they require cleaning this must be done carefully to ensure that the seatings are not scratched or otherwise damaged.

Insert the new valve with the " dome " pointing inwards so that the small centre seat of the valve is resting in contact with the centre seat of the valve holder. If the new valve is the Mk. II pattern (green colour) a check plate must be fitted on top of the valve before the valve guard is replaced.

Replace the valve guard on the centre pin of the valve holder and screw up the captive nut with the fingers as far as possible. Finally tighten up half a turn with the securing key *held in the fingers. On no account must a tool be used to obtain extra leverage on the key.*

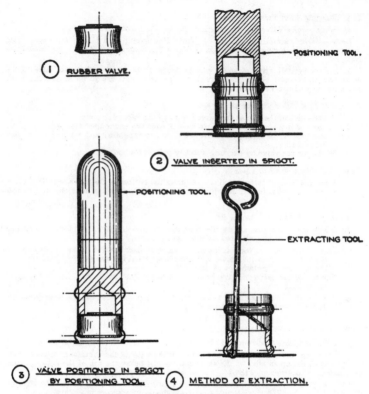

1. RUBBER VALVE.

2. VALVE INSERTED IN SPIGOT.

POSITIONING TOOL.

POSITIONING TOOL.

EXTRACTING TOOL

3. VALVE POSITIONED IN SPIGOT BY POSITIONING TOOL.

4. METHOD OF EXTRACTION.

FIG. 5.—INLET VALVE NO. 4. (CONTAINER TYPE E)

S. 6. Changing Eyepiece Discs (S. type fitted with detachable rims).

Materials.—Splinterless glass discs: Eyepiece washers: Mineral jelly.

Tool.—Eyepiece removal tool.

The procedure is the same as for the eyepieces of C.D. respirators—see C.D. 6 in Part 4.

S. 7. Repairs to Stockinette (S. type).

Materials.—Rubber solution.

The edges of the stockinette covering of Service type facepieces or connecting tubes which become detached may be re-secured by application of rubber solution to the detached surfaces of the fabric, the solution being allowed to become thoroughly tacky before the fabric is stuck down.

S. 8. Repairs to Haversacks (S. type).

Materials.—Whipcord; thread (khaki or buff); "D" loops (9/16″ and 1″): "S" hooks; spring hooks; slides.

Tools.—Needles; scissors.

Simple repairs to haversacks, including replacement of metal fittings as noted above, repair of seams, and replacement of whipcord may be carried out.

Arrangements may also be made with the local traders for replacement of snap fasteners, an operation which requires the use of suitable closing tools. Such repair will usually require provision of reinforcing fabric where the old fastener has become detached.

Summary of Materials and Tools for Repair of Respirators

Except where marked for local purchase, the following materials and tools will be supplied by the Ministry of Home Security.

I. *Materials.*

Nomenclature	Type of Respirator
Check Plate Mk. I	S.
Disc, Eyepiece, C.D. Mk. I	C.D.
Disc, Eyepiece, 2½″ Mk. II	S.
Elastic Webbing ¼″	C.D., S.
Hook, " S," Haversack Mk. V or VI	S.
Hook, Spring, Haversack Mk. V or VI	S.
Loop, Mk. I C.D.	C.D. ⎫
Loop, Mk. II S.	S. ⎬ interchangeable.
Loop, " D," ⁹⁄₁₆″	S.
Loop, " D," 1″	S.
Pad, Harness	C.D., S.
Pin, Safety	G.C.
Rubber Band	G.C.
Screw, Tail-piece (B.H.)	B.H.
Slide, Haversack Mk. V or VI	S.
Tag, Mk. I, C.D.	C.D. ⎫
Tag, Mk. II, S.	S. ⎬ interchangeable
Tape, Adhesive, ½″ (white)	S.
Tape, Adhesive, ¾″	B.H.
Tape, Adhesive, 1″	for Contex
Toggle Clip, C.D.	C.D.
Valve Inlet No. 1 (black rubber)	G.C., B.H., C.D.
do. (red rubber)	S.C.
Valve Inlet No. 3A or No. 4	S.
Valve Outlet No. 2 Mk. I or Mk. II	S.
Washer, Eyepiece	C.D., S.
Whipcord	C.D., S.
Wire, Binding, 11″	S.
For local purchase—	
Mineral Jelly	C.D., S.
Rubber Patches	G.C., S.C., B.H.
Rubber Solution	G.C., S.C., B.H., S.
Thread	C.D., S.
Tape (woven)	B.H.

II. *Tools.*

Nomenclature	Type of Respirator
Container Detaching Tool	S.
Eyepiece Removal Tool	C.D., S.
Valve Guard Securing Key Mk. I	S.
Valve Extractor Mk. I	S.
Valve Extractor Mk. II	S.
Valve Positioning Tool Mk. I	S.
Valve Positioning Tool Mk. III	S.
For local purchase—	
Hammer 8 oz. (1″ face)	C.D., S.
Needles	C.D., S.
Pliers, side cutting 6″ or 8″	C.D., S.
Scissors	C.D., S.

APPENDIX C.

INSTRUCTIONS FOR REPAIR OF OILSKIN GARMENTS MADE OF FABRIC D.

I. *Materials.*

Fabric D, for patches.
Strips of fabric D, on which male and female portions of press fasteners have been mounted.
Dope (in tins), for restoring the oil film.

II. *Tools.*

Sewing machine (household machines are adequate) (for local provision).
Small nail brushes (for local provision).

1. Heavy oilskin jackets and trousers.
No local repairs are authorised.

2. Light oilskin jackets and trousers, hoods and curtains (all made of fabric D).
The following repairs are to be carried out locally.

(1) *Patching tears.*—

(*a*) Straight tears of any length may be repaired, provided that they end not less than 2 inches from any existing seams. Other tears may be repaired under the special authorisation of the officer in charge of the Depot—e.g. a tear at a point on a hem or seam where a satisfactory gas-tight patch can be securely applied, and dog-legged tears not in a vital position. Tears coming within 2 inches of seams in the shoulder area of jackets, or the fork of trousers, should not be repaired locally.

(*b*) The fabric used for patching must be fabric D material. Garments must not be cut up locally to provide patches.

(*c*) The ordinary household sewing machine is suitable for stitching the patches.

(*d*) The edges of the patches are to be turned under and sewn down. The edge of the patch must never be closer to the tear than 1 inch. The raw edges of the tear are to be stitched to the patch on both sides.

(*e*) After the repair has been made, all new seams should be well doped on both sides, and the dope allowed to dry thoroughly before the garment is returned to use or store (see (3) below).

(2) *Replacing damaged or missing press fasteners.*—The repair consists of the removal of damaged studs and stitching into position a patch with the requisite portion cut from the strip described above. It will be noted that in the case of the male portion the patch should simply be placed over the hole where the missing portion was fixed. In the case of the female portion the spot where the missing part was fixed must be cut out before patching.
If the portion of the new fastener does not fit the other portion already on the garment, that portion too must be replaced.

(3) *Doping rubbed or cracked surfaces.*—Where the oil film has been damaged on *small* areas by abrasion or folding, but the fabric is not torn and the garment is otherwise in good condition, repair may be carried out by recoating with dope. This may be done on both sides where necessary. A thin coat only should be applied with a small nail brush, and the dope allowed to dry. Several thin coats should be applied if one is not sufficient.
The dope will take from 1 to 2 days to dry under normal weather conditions, but drying can be accelerated by hanging the garments in a chamber in which the air is heated to not more than 120° F. (In this connection attention is drawn to the danger of naked lights near oilskin.)
If a supply of dope is not available, boiled linseed oil may be used instead. This will take a longer time to dry.

3. Oilskin Gloves.

Small abrasions or cracks in the oil film may be repaired by doping on both sides when necessary. Patching of gloves should not be attempted locally.

B10792. Wt.1850. 15,000. 8/40. U.B.L. G428.   S.O. Code No. 34-9999.